EMPLOYEE WORK PLACE STRESS

[A study of Middle level Employees of Sabar Dairy]

AUTHOR

Dr. Darshin R. Upadhyay

:: PUBLICATION ::

**Shree Avadhut Education Trust
Himatnagar, Sabarkantha,
Gujrat-383001**

ISBN 978-93-84485-87-0

ISBN 978-93-84485-87-0

First Publication
December - 2015
Typing & Design
Bharat B. Patel
Excellence Computer, Himatnagar
Printing & Binding
Manohar Book Binding, Himatnagar

: PUBLISHED BY :
**Shree Avadhut Education Trust
Himatnagar**
Sabarkantha, Gujrat-383001

Price: Rs.225/-

Dedicated To ....

My wife & Krishna

: INDEX :

CHAPTER-I
INTRODUCTION

Introduction

Stress in the workplace is a growing concern in the current state of the economy, where employees increasingly face conditions of overwork, job insecurity, low levels of job satisfaction, and lack of autonomy. Workplace stress has been shown to have a detrimental effect on the health and well¬being of employees, as well as a negative impact on workplace productivity and profits. There are measures that individuals and organizations can take to alleviate the negative impact of stress, or to stop it from arising in the first place. However, employees first need to learn to recognize the signs that indicate they are feeling stressed out, and employers need to be aware of the effects that stress has on their employees health as well as on company profits.

Concept of Stress

Stress means some imbalance between the person developed, particularly that surrounding the person-environment (P-E) interaction, researches have considered the nature of that interaction and, more importantly, the psychological processes which it takes place (Dewey, 1992).

Stress is a physiological and psychological imbalance. It arises due to the demands on a person and that person's inability to meet these demands. Stress is the body's way of reacting to any situation and it can have serious repercussions on an individual's life. Yet, people fail to realize the importance of stress management in their lives. Effective managers can stay in control of life, without panicking even under stressful situations. They handle stress by planning work, taking regular breaks, and rejuvenating them.

Stress: Meaning and Definitions

Stress is a word derived from the Latin word 'Stringer', meaning todraw tight and was used in the seventeenth century to describe hardship or affliction. During the late eighteenth century, stress denoted 'force, pressure, strain, or strong effort', referring primarily to an individual or to the individual's organs or mental power.

Hans Selye's view in 1956 was that "stress is not necessarily something bad – it all depends on how you take it. The stress of exhilarating, creative successful work is beneficial, while that of failure, humiliation or infection is detrimental."Selye believed that the biochemical effects of stress would be experienced irrespective of whether the situation was positive or negative.

Defining stress - The wider the usage of the term 'stress', the more elusive its meaning. Modern definitions of stress all recognize that it is a personal experience caused by pressure or demands on an individual, and impacts upon the individual's ability to cope or rather, his/her perception of that ability.

The term 'stress' has a different meaning for researchers in various disciplines. In the biological literature, it is used in relation to single organisms, populations of organisms, and ecosystems. Biologists refer to things such as heat, cold and inadequate food supply as being sources of stress. Human biologists add to this microbial infection and taking toxic substances. Social scientists, for their part, are more concerned about people's interaction with their environment and the resulting emotional disturbances that can sometimes accompany it (Hinkle, 1987).

The term stress has many definitions (Lazarus & Folk man, 1984). We all define stress as an internal state which can be caused by physical demands on the body (disease conditions, exercise, extremes of temperature, and the like) or by environmental and social situations which a evaluated as potentially, harmful, uncontrollable, or exceeding resources for coping. The physical, environmental, and social causes of the stress state are termed stressors.

Stress in individuals is defined as anything that disrupts the normal person's physical or mental well-being. It occurs when the body performs activities outside its capabilities or when a person faces extraordinary demands. A simple display of stress may be a bad mood while an extreme display may be an act of violence. The process of stress has a stressor or a stimulus. A stressor is a factor or stimulant that creates stress. A stressor is not in itself either positive or negative or good or bad, it is how one reacts to it that determines its positivity or negativity. For example, one person may perceive stressor as a motivator,

3

whereas another person may perceive it as a constraint. One individual may perceive it as a challenge, another as a threat.

Stress can be positive or negative. Positive stress is called estruses and negative stress is called distress. There is a difference between the ways in which estruses and distress affect the body. Estruses triggers the body alarm, enhances attention, performance, and creativity. It has temporary effects. For instance, a person applying for a visa to the US may be under estruses, and once he/she obtains the visa his/her stress levels come back to normal. Distress has a negative effect on the body. For instance, an individual who has lost his/her job may become depressed, which is a result of distress. Distress, if left unchecked, can have a serious effect on the body over a period of time. The body's nonspecific response to the external situation results in stress and stress can create a number of health problems both mental and physical. Some of these problems are sleeplessness, eating disorders, heart problems, and suicidal tendencies. Stress represents the wear and tear of the human body.

A certain level of stress can act as a motivator. Without stress, a person becomes lethargic and dull. Good stress encourages a person to perform better. However, if this stress exceeds the resistance level of the individual, it can turn into distress. The perception of stress varies from person to person and each person has his/her own stress limit. There are many reasons and sources of stress for every person. Also, while some people tend to work better under pressure, there are others who cannot bear the 'last minute syndrome.' They panic when faced with even the most minor of stressful situations.

What is stress? We are all familiar with the word "stress". Stress is when you are worried about getting laid off your job, or worried about having enough money to pay your bills, or worried about your mother when the doctor says she may need as operation. In fact, to most of us, stress is synonymous with worry. If it is something that makes you worry, then it is stress.

Your body, however, has a much broader definition of stress. To your body, stress is synonymous with change. Anything that causes a change in your life causes stress. It doesn't matter if it is a "good" change, or a "bad" change, they are both stress. When you find your dream apartment and get ready to move, that is stress. If you break your leg, that is stress. Good or bad, if it is a change in your life, it is stress as far as your body is concerned.

Even imagines change is stress. Imagining changes is what we call "worrying".) If you fear that you will not have enough money to pay your rent, that is stress, if you worry that you may get fired, that is stress. If you think that you may receive a promotion at work, which is also stress (even though this would be a good change). Whether the event is good or bad, imagining changes in your life is stressful. Anything that causes change in your body health is stressful. Imagines changes are just as stressful as real changes.

STRESS...AT WORK

A recent report by the National Association of Mental Health distinguishes between stress and pressure, where pressure can be defined as a subjective feeling of tension or arousal that is triggered by a potentially stressful situation. However, where pressure exceeds an individual's ability to cope, the result is stress.

Explaining stress - The HSE has identified six categories of substantive factors that can be identified as potential causes of work-related stress:

- Demands
- Control
- Relationships
- Change
- Role
- Support.

Another potential risk factor is work-life balance. A 'vicious cycle' can occur when mounting stress in one area of life spills over and makes coping with the other yet more difficult. Palmer et al developed a model of work-related stress that helped to inform the HSE (health and safety executive) approach. This added a seventh driver of stress – culture – which is defined as 'the culture of the organization and how it approaches and manages work-related stress when it arises'.

Although the experience of stress is subjective, and is mediated by the personal evaluation of a situation by the individual, there are nevertheless a number of substantive factors that can be identified as potential causes of work-related stress. These, of course, will vary in degree and importance depending on the particular job, but theHSE has identified six categories of potential stressors:

Demands: This includes factors intrinsic to the job such as working conditions (for example noise, temperature, lighting or ventilation), shift work, long or unsociable hours, workload.

Control: How much say and autonomy a person has over the way in which he carries out his job; low levels of job control are typically linked to high levels of stress.

Relationships: Relationships with superiors, subordinates and colleagues can all play a part in an individual's stress levels; low levels of trust and support are likely to increase stress. Also, conflict, harassment and bullying in the workplace are all linked to heightened stress.

Change: The way in which change is introduced, managed and communicated to staff can impact on levels of stress, as unnecessary or badly planned change results in excess pressure on workers.

Role: Stress may be triggered when an individual does not have a clear understanding of his role within the organization, when there is conflict between roles or ambiguity with regards to position and degree of responsibility over others.

Support: The amount of support and job training available, as well as encouragement, sponsorship and resources provided by colleagues and management.

Another potential risk factor not included in the six HSE categories of stressors is the interface between work and home, often referred to as the work-life balance. Individuals who work long, uncertain or unsocial hours may find it difficult to juggle the competing demands of work and domestic pressures, particularly if they have children or other dependents. This can lead to a 'vicious cycle' in which mounting stress in one area of life spills over and makes coping with the other yet more difficult.

Utilizing these potential stress risk factors, Palmer et al have developed a model of work-related stress that has helped to inform the HSE's current approach to stress management and prevention, and is indicated by the diagram below. It should be noted that in this model a further, seventh driver of stress is identified – culture – which is not identified as an explicit stressor by the HSE but which Palmer et al describe as 'the culture of the organization and how it approaches and manages work-related stress when it arises'.

Workplace Stress

Workplace stress is the harmful physical and emotional response that occurs when there is a poor match between job demands and the capabilities, Resources, or needs of the worker. Stress-related disorders encompass a broad Array of conditions, including psychological disorders (e.g., depression, anxiety, Post-traumatic stress disorder) and other types of emotional strain (e.g., dissatisfaction, fatigue, tension, etc.), maladaptive behaviors (e.g., aggression, Substance abuse), and cognitive impairment (e.g., concentration and memory).

Health and Healthcare Utilization

Problems at work are more strongly associated with health complaints than are any other life stressor-more so than even financial problems or family problems. Many studies suggest that psychologically demanding jobs that allow employees little control over the work process increases the risk of cardiovascular disease. On the basis of research by the National Institute for Occupational Safety and Health and many other organizations, it is widely believed that job stress increases the risk for development of back and upper-extremity musculoskeletalDisorders. High levels of stress are associated with substantial increases in Health service utilization. Workers who report experiencing stress at work also show excessive health care utilization. In a 1998 study of 46,000 workers, health care costs were nearly 50% greater for workers reporting high levels of stress in Comparison to "low risk" workers. The increment rose to nearly 150%, an increase of more than $1,700 per person annually, for workers reporting highLevels of both stress and depression. Additionally, periods of disability due to job stress tend to be much longer than disability periods for other occupational Injuries and illnesses.

Causes of Workplace Stress

Job stress results from the interaction of the worker and the conditions of work. Views differ on the importance of worker characteristics versus working conditions as the primary cause of job stress. The differing viewpoints suggest different ways to prevent stress at work. According to one school of thought, differences in individual characteristics such as personality and coping skills are most important in predicting whether certain job conditions will result in stress-inother words, what is stressful for one person may not be a problem for someone else. This viewpoint leads to prevention strategies that focus on workers and ways to help them cope with demanding job conditions. Although the importance of individual differences cannot be ignored, scientific evidence suggests that certain working conditions are stressful to most people. Such evidence argues for a greater emphasis on working conditions as the key source of job stress, and for job redesign as a primary prevention strategy. Personal interview surveys of working conditions, including conditions recognized as risk factors for job stress, were conducted in Member States of the European Union in 1990, 1995, and 2000. Results showed a trend across these periods suggestive of increasing work intensity. In 1990, the percentage of workers reporting that they worked at high speeds at least one-fourth of their working time was 48%, increasing to 54% in 1995 and to 56% in 2000. Similarly, 50% of workers reported they work against tight deadlines at least one-fourth of their working time in 1990, increasing to 56% in 1995 and 60 % in 2000. However, no change was noted in the period 1995–2000 (data not collected in 1990) in the percentage of workers reporting sufficient time to complete tasks. A substantial percentage of Americans work very long hours. By one estimate, more than 26% of men and more than 11% of women worked 50 hours per week or more in 2000. These figures represent a considerable increase over the previous three decades, especially for women. According to the Department of Labor, there has been an upward trend in hours worked among employed women, an increase in extended work weeks (>40 hours) by men, and a considerable increase in combined working hours among working couples, particularly couples with young children.

Signs of Workplace Stress

Mood and sleep disturbances, upset stomach and headache, and disturbed relationships with family; friends and girlfriends or boyfriends are examples of stress-related problems. The effects of job stress on chronic diseases are more difficult to see because chronic diseases take a long time to develop and can be influenced by many factors other than stress. Nonetheless, evidence is rapidly accumulating to suggest that stress plays an important role in several types of chronic health problems-especially cardiovascular disease, musculoskeletal disorders, and psychological disorders.

Prevention

A combination of organizational change and stress management is often the most useful approach for preventing stress at work. How to Change the Organization to Prevent Job Stress. Ensure that the workload is in line with workers' capabilities and resources. Design jobs to provide meaning, stimulation, and opportunities for workers to use their skills, clearly define workers' roles and responsibilities. Give workers opportunities to participate in decisions and actions affecting their jobs. Improve communications-reduce uncertainty about career development and future employment prospects. Provide opportunities for social interaction among workers. Establish work schedules that are compatible with demands and responsibilities outside the job. Discrimination inside the workplace. (E.g. nationality and language) St. Paul Fire and Marine Insurance Company conducted several studies on the effects of stress prevention programs in hospital settings. Program activities included (1) employee and management education on job stress, (2) changes in hospital policies and procedures to reduce organizational sources of stress, and (3) establishment of employee assistance programs. In one study, the frequency of medication errors declined by 50% after prevention activities was implemented in a 700-bed hospital. In a second study, there was a 70% reduction in malpractice claims in 22 hospitals that implemented stress prevention activities.

In contrast, there was no reduction in claims in a matched group of 22 hospitals that did not implement stress prevention activities.

Reduce your stress
1. **Job analysis: -**

We have all experienced that appalling sense of having far too much work to do and too little time to do it in. We can choose to ignore this, and work unreasonably long hours to stay on top of our workload. The risks here are that we become exhausted, that we have so much to do that we do a poor quality job and that we neglect other areas of our life. Each of these can lead to intense stress. The alternative is to work more intelligently, by focusing on the things that are important for job success and reducing the time we spend on low priority tasks.

Job Analysis is the first step in doing this. The first of the action-oriented skills that we look at is Job Analysis. Job Analysis is a key technique for managing job overload – an important source of stress. To do an excellent job, you need to fully understand what is expected of you. While this may seem obvious, in the hurly-burly of a new, fast-moving, high pressure role, it is oftentimes something that is easy to overlook. By understanding the priorities in your job, and what constitutes success within it, you can focus on these activities and minimize work on other tasks as much as possible. This helps you get the greatest return from the work you do, and keep your workload under control. Job Analysis is a useful technique for getting a firm grip on what really is important in your job so that you are able to perform excellently. It helps you to cut through clutter and distraction to get to the heart of what you need to do.

2. **Rational & positive thinking: -**

You are thinking negatively when you fear the future, put yourself down, criticize yourself for errors, doubt your abilities, or expect failure. Negative thinking damages confidence, harms performance and paralyzes mental skills. Unfortunately, negative thoughts tend to flit into our consciousness, do their damage and flit back out again, with their significance having barely been noticed. Since we barely realize that they were there, we do not challenge them properly, which means that they can be completely incorrect and wrong. Thought Awareness is the process by which you observe your thoughts and become aware of what is going through your head.

One approach to it is to observe your "stream of consciousness" as you think about the thing you're trying to achieve which is stressful. Do not suppress any thoughts. Instead, just let them run their course while you watch them, and write them down on our free worksheet as they occur. Then let them go. Another more general approach to Thought Awareness comes with logging stress in your Stress Diary. When you analyze your diary at the end of the period, you should be able to see the most common and the most damaging thoughts. Tackle these as a priority using the techniques below. Here are some typical negative thoughts you might experience when preparing to give a major presentation: · Fear about the quality of your performance or of problems that may interfere with it; Worry about how the audience (especially important people in it like your boss) or the press may react to you; Dwelling on the negative consequences of a poor performance; or Self-criticism over a less-than-perfect rehearsal.

Thought awareness is the first step in the process of managing negative thoughts, as you cannot manage thoughts that you are unaware of.

Rational Thinking

The next step in dealing with negative thinking is to challenge the negative thoughts that you identified using the Thought Awareness technique. Look at every thought you wrote down and challenge it rationally. Ask yourself whether the thought is reasonable. What evidence is there for and against the thought? Would your colleagues and mentors agree or disagree with it?

Looking at the examples, the following challenges could be made to the negative thoughts we identified earlier:

· **Feelings of inadequacy:** Have you trained yourself as well as you reasonably should have? Do you have the experience and resources you need to make the presentation? Have you planned, prepared and rehearsed enough? If you have done all of these, you've done as much as you can to give a good performance.

· **Worries about performance during rehearsal:** If some of your practice was less than perfect, then remind yourself that the purpose of the practice is to identify areas for improvement, so that these can be sorted out before the performance.

· **Problems with issues outside your control:** Have you identified the risks of these things happening, and have you taken steps to reduce the likelihood of them happening or their impact if they do? What will you do if they occur? And what do you need others to do for you?

· **Worry about other people's reactions:** If you have prepared well, and you do the best you can, then you should be satisfied. If you perform as well as you reasonably can, then fair people are likely to respond well. If people are not fair, the best thing to do is ignore their comments and rise above them.

Tip:
Don't make the mistake of generalizing a single incident. OK, you made a mistake at work, but that doesn't mean you're bad at your job. Similarly, make sure you take the long view about incidents that you're finding stressful. Just because you're finding these new responsibilities stressful now, doesn't mean that they will ALWAYS be so for you in the future.

Tip:

If you find it difficult to look at your negative thoughts objectively, imagine that you are your best friend or a respected coach or mentor. Look at the list of negative thoughts and imagine the negative thoughts were written by someone you were giving objective advice to. Then, think how you would challenge these thoughts. When you challenge negative thoughts rationally, you should be able to see quickly whether the thoughts are wrong or whether they have some substance to them. Where there is some substance, take appropriate action. However, make sure that your negative thoughts are genuinely important to achieving your goals, and don't just reflect a lack of experience, which everyone has to go through at some stage.

Positive Thinking & Opportunity Seeking

By now, you should already be feeling more positive. The final step is to prepare rational, positive thoughts and affirmations to counter any remaining negativity. It can also be useful to look at the situation and see if there are any useful opportunities that are offered by it. By basing your affirmations on the clear, rational assessments of facts that you made using Rational Thinking, you can use them to undo the damage that negative thinking may have done to your self-confidence.

Tip:

Your affirmations will be strongest if they are specific, are expressed in the present tense and have strong emotional content. Continuing the examples above, positive affirmations might be:

Problems during practice: "I have learned from my rehearsals. This has put me in a position where I can deliver a great performance. I am going to perform well and enjoy the event."

Worries about performance: "I have prepared well and rehearsed thoroughly. I am well positioned to give an excellent performance."

Problems issues outside your control: "I have thought through everything that might reasonably happen and have planned how I can handle all likely contingencies. I am very well placed to react flexibly to events."

Worry about other people's reaction: "Fair people will react well to a good performance. I will rise above any unfair criticism in a mature and professional way." If appropriate, write these affirmations down on your worksheet so that you can use them when you need them. As well as allowing you to structure useful affirmations, part of Positive Thinking is to look at opportunities that the situation might offer to you. In the examples above, successfully overcoming the situations causing the original negative thinking will open up opportunities. You will acquire new skills, you will be seen as someone who can handle difficult challenges, and you may open up new career opportunities. Make sure that identifying these opportunities and focusing on them is part of your positive thinking.

❖ **The relationship between stress and pressure**

Everyone experiences pressure at some time in his or her life. Pressure is not only inevitable but essential to help us feel stimulated and excited about achieving the goals that give us our sense of achievement and satisfaction.

Problems arise only when pressure is excessive, prolonged or come from too many directions at the same time. This excessive pressure challenges our ability to cope by creating a feeling of being out of control. Most people can deal with high levels of pressure at times, but when additional pressures or crises arise it may become increasingly difficult, if not impossible, to cope.

To manage occupational stress, the importance of personal and domestic problems must be recognized. Sometimes it is difficult to be certain where to start, as difficulties at work may make a personal problem more acute, and vice versa. There are a number of factors that can explain some of the individual differences in susceptibility to pressure; these include:

- Competence in doing the job
- Lifestyle
- Personality
- Ability and opportunity to relax
- Personal susceptibility
- Support and training at work
- Physical health and fitness
- Support from family and friends.

There are immediate and longer-term responses to excessive pressure. The acute reactions are related to arousal and involve feelings of anxiety, a racing pulse, flushing, sweating, a dry mouth and trembling. If the pressure goes on for a longer period of time the reactions can include headaches, inability to sleep, skin conditions, a sudden loss or gain in weight, aching muscles and depression.

Long-term pressure can lead to physical and psychological illness or may make existing medical conditions, such as heart disease, worse.

Work performance	Emotional behavior
Inability to concentrate	Crying
Loss of enthusiasm	Aggressive behavior
Declining/inconsistent performance	Over-reaction to problems
Failing to take annual leave	Sudden mood changes
Accidents	Irritability/moodiness
Withdrawal	**Relationships**
Reluctance to give or offer support	Criticism of others

Arriving late and leaving early	Lack of co-operation
Extended lunches	Marital or family difficulties
Absenteeism	Poor employee relations

❖ Stress and ill-health –

There are clear links between work-related stress and a variety of physical and mental disorders, despite the difficulty of proving a direct causal link since the majority of diseases and syndromes commonly attributed to stress have multiple causes. The effects of work-related stress on ill-health operate in physiological, cognitive, emotional and behavioral ways.

The word 'stress' now forms part of most people's daily vocabulary but its reach and meaning remain unclear. Whilst the report starts off by providing a series of working definitions around stress, and charting its changing meanings, it goes on to look at more quantitative evidence in order to shed light on the divergence between popular discourses and a more robust, evidence-driven understanding of stress.

The effects of work-related stress on ill-health operate in a number of ways:

- o **Physiologically:** nervousness, endocrinal or immunological reactions within the body can lead to symptoms of physical and mental illness.
- o **Cognitively:** working conditions and situations are interpreted by the individual as 'stressful' and therefore pathogenic.
- o **Emotionally:** seemingly trivial incidents are experienced as debilitating, dangerous, or even life-threatening.
- o **Behaviourally:** excessive work strain encourages potentially damaging behaviours, such as smoking, alcoholism, eating disorders, or self-harm.

- **Physical ill-health**

The immediate effect of stress on the body is to trigger a natural biological response to challenging or threatening events – frequently referred to as the 'fight or flight' response. When the individual encounters a potential stressor, blood flow is redirected from the skin and internal organs to the muscles and the brain; glucose and fatty acids are mobilized into the bloodstream to provide energy; vision and hearing are sharpened and alertness is increased. The functioning of routine bodily maintenance such as digestion, restorative processes and the immune system are all reduced. Although this stress response is a normal, evolutionary reaction to a perceived threat, when it occurs frequently or is prolonged, intense or poorly managed, it can pose a risk to health.

The suppression of the immune system under chronic stress leads to the 'general adaptation syndrome' which results in a generalized risk of greater susceptibility to illness and disease. Depending on the vulnerabilities of the individual in question, it may also contribute to a range of medical, psychological and behavioural disorders, all of which are detrimental not only to physical and mental well-being, but also to job performance, productivity, absence levels and staff turnover.

When stressful situations are not resolved and persist for some time, the body is kept in a constant state of alertness and defensive action, increasing wear and tear on biological systems, resulting in damage and exhaustion. During the 'fight or flight' response, the immune system is weakened, increasing vulnerability to illness and compromising the body's ability to repair itself and defend itself against disease. Short term symptoms include headaches, muscular tension, chest pains, indigestion, palpitations, disturbed sleep and increased susceptibility to respiratory infections. Long term illnesses attributable to work-related stress include heart disease, hypertension, ulcers, irritable bowel syndrome, high cholesterol and increased risk of cancer, diabetes and asthma.

Although work-related stress alone probably does not cause cancer, it is known to contribute to a number of stress-related behaviors that secondarily increase the risk of developing cancer. In particular, these include: smoking, excessive alcohol consumption, overeating or consuming too much fatty food.

- **Mental ill-health**
There is a strong relationship between work-related stress and mental ill-health – excessive and persistent stress can trigger

and escalate mental illness. Psychological problems that are frequently brought on by work-related stress include: fatigue, low self-esteem, irritability, depressive and acute anxiety disorders and posttraumatic stress disorder.

MIND (2005) states that *perceived* job stress is essential to understanding and explaining the worker's mental health11, in other words, explanations do not reside solely in the existence of objective work stressors such as shift work or long working hours. This is not to say that the stressed worker is responsible for his own plight, but rather that working conditions and individual perceptions of those conditions must be understood together. Most importantly, the views and experience of the person suffering stress should be acknowledged and taken seriously.

The research undertaken by MIND suggests that certain perceptions of job stress are more likely than others to lead to psychological problems such as anxiety or depression. These aspects include: a perception of a 'poor relationship with a superior' or a perception of 'too much trouble at work'. There also appears to be a heightened risk of employees suffering from a psychiatric disorder when they have little say or control over how their work is done; when their work is fast paced; has conflicting priorities or when they feel there is a lack of recognition, understanding and support from managers.

The effects of psychiatric disorders brought about by work-related stress are significant, both for the individual concerned and for the employer. Anxiety, depression and other emotional problems commonly lead to sickness absence, medical consultations and treatment and high levels of suffering and dysfunction.

In sum, though the word 'stress' now forms part of most people's daily vocabulary, its reach and meaning remain unclear. In popular usage, stress is used to describe individual responses to innumerable everyday pressures, as well as to larger life events. In addition, stress is frequently seen as an important factor in the development of a range of psychological and physical ailments. At the workplace, the term is now widely deployed.

The below table showing the effects of stress on bodily functions.

	Normal (relaxed)	**Under pressure**	**Acute pressure**	**Chronic pressure (stress)**
Brain	Blood supply Normal	Blood supply increased	Thinks more clearly	Headaches or migraines, tremors and nervous tics
Mood	Happy	Serious	Increased concentration	Anxiety, loss of sense of humour
Saliva	Normal	Reduced	Reduced	Dry mouth, lump in throat
Muscles	Blood supply	Blood supply	Improved performance	Muscular tension

	Normal	increased		and pain
Heart	Normal rate and blood pressure	Increased rate and blood pressure	Improved performance	Hypertension and chest pains
Lungs	Normal respiration rate	Increased respiration rate	Improved performance	Coughs and asthma
Stomach	Normal blood supply and acid secretion	Reduced blood supply and increased acid secretion	Reduced blood supply reduces digestion	Ulcers due to heartburn and indigestion
Bowels	Normal blood supply and bowel activity	Reduced blood supply and increased bowel activity	Reduced blood supply reduces digestion	Abdominal pain and diarrhoea
Bladder	Normal	Frequent urination	Frequent urination due to increased nervous stimulation	Frequent urination, prostatic symptoms
Sexual organs	Male: Normal Female: Normal periods etc.	Male: Impotence (decreased blood supply) Female: Irregular periods	Decreased blood supply	Male: Impotence Female: Menstrual disorders

Skin	Healthy	Decreased blood supply, dry skin	Decreased blood supply	Dryness and rashes
Biochemistry	Normal – oxygen consumed, glucose and fats liberated	Oxygen consumption increased, glucose and fat consumption increased	More energy immediately available	Rapid tiredness

Source: Melhuish, Executive Health

By both management and workforce to describe Individual and collective experiences of fatigue, distress and an inability to cope with the demands of work.

Conclusion

This section has provided a series of working definitions and charted the changing meanings and usages of 'stress.' In the following section we turn to more quantitative evidence in order to examine the latest facts and figures on occupational stress. This evidence sheds further light on the divergence between popular discourses and a more robust, evidence driven understanding of stress.

CHAPTER-II
REVIEW OF LITERATURE

A review of literature is a must for scientific approach and regarded to be by and large important for research, it gives the investigator an understanding of the previous work having been done related to present study. One cannot develop an insight into the various facts of problems unless and until one has learnt the previous theories. Research is concerned with the systematic gathering of information. Its purpose is to help in the research for truth.

The purpose of this chapter is to provide a brief and initial review and appraisal of the related studies and to see what present study contributes more knowledge further in the areas under study.

• International Level:

French & Caplan (1970) found at one of NASA's bases in a sample of 205, found role ambiguity in volunteer engineers, scientists and administrators was related to low job satisfaction and to the feeling of job related to threat to one's mental physical well-being. This is also related to indicators of physiological strain such as increased blood pressure and pulse rate.

The finding of **Lazarus and Folk man (1980),** also substantiate the discussion that work stress will generate among human beings where a particular relationship between the person and the environment, that is appraised by the person as taxing or exceeding his/her resources and endangering his/her well being. The situation of non-nationalized bank employees is similar to the above-mentioned findings of eminent researchers. Where there is high uncertainty about their nature of work, develop high job stress among members.

The study indicates that the non-nationalized bank employees have high ambiguity compared to nationalize bank employees. Higher the ambiguity related to the work and work schedule higher the occupational stress. The role ambiguity results when there low congruity between the expectations of the work behavior and the scheduled task. There is lack of clarity about what to do, when to do, where to do and how to do. Experimental and longitudinal studies of the effects of role ambiguity reveal that lack of clarity about behavioural expectations causes a great concern with own performance, lower actual and perceived group productivity, less concern or involvement with the group, lower job satisfaction, unfavorable attitudes towards role senders, and increased tension, anxiety, depression, and resentment (Caplan and Jones, 1975). The present research is in line with the above finding that the members of non-nationalized members are facing high role ambiguity at work because of lack of clarity about behavioural expectations on work. Higher the level of ambiguity, higher the level of stress experienced by members at work. Lack of free flow information all across the hierarchical level, is the problem lead to role ambiguity at work. Role ambiguity exists when an individual has inadequate information about his work role.

The study indicates that the non-nationalized bank employees have high feeling towards lack of supervisory support compared to nationalize bank employees. This indicates that the non-nationalized bank employees are not getting adequate support from the superiors in their work accomplishments and dissemination of functional duties. Lower the level of support employees obtained from the organization higher the level of stress experienced by the employees at work. The superior's contribution to buffer the effect of work stress is found less in this research.

Paul (1971) founded the demands of combing work and family roles to be highly stressful and exhausting. At the same time dual careers provides the opportunity for multiple sources of satisfaction from both partners (Crosby, 1984). The demands of dual careers family are not necessarily greater than those of traditional family they are just different. The second work-family conflict, i.e. strain-based conflict, arises when strain in one role affects one's performance in another role. The third is behavior- based conflict, which refers to incompatibility between the behavior patterns that are desirable in the two domains.

The results of study by **Eden, Silbrwasser& Keller man (1973)** on different occupational groups: showed the managerial & professional occupations are more likely to suffer occupational stress from role-related stress & other interpersonal dynamics & less from the physical conditions of work.

Mc Murray (1973) is of the view that over promoted manager suffers from "execute neurosis", hence over-works to keep his position & also tries to hide his insecurity & feeling.

Kearns (1973) is of the view that stress can be caused due to fatigue from the physical strains of the work environment, excessive travel, long hours, having to cope with change at work and the expenses (monetary and career) of making mistakes.

Kay (1974) said that irrespective of employing organizational middle managers experience job insecurity as a result of higher responsibility, but little authority & limited salary as compared to new recruit higher risks of developing symptoms of stress because they are distant from the top & have little influence on decision- making & at the same time are too close to the junior management.

Middle managers experience pressures from many directions top (supervisor), bottom (subordinates) & lateral (colleagues). They are sometimes unable to balance their relationship with their subordinates & supervisor, they have to take the approval of their superiors before initiating any action plan, they consults & co-ordinates with their colleagues over whom they have no formal contracts & finally organize the execution of the plan by delegating to their subordinates. Social support in form of approval from superiors, co-ordination from colleagues and co-ordination from subordinates is not able to cope with these pressures.

Margoles (1974) found a number of significant relationship between symptoms or indicators of physical and mental ill Health with role ambiguity were depressed mood, lowered self-esteem, life dissatisfaction, and low motivation to work and intent to leaving the job.

According to **French and Caplan (1975),** "Pressure of both qualitative and quantitative overload can result in the need to work excessive hours, which is an additional source of stress." Having to work under time pressure in order to meet deadlines is an independent source of stress. Studies show that stress levels increase as difficult deadlines draw near.

Stress is often developed when an individual is assigned a major responsibility without proper authority and delegation of power. Interpersonal factors such as group cohesiveness, functional dependence, communication frequency, relative authority and organizational distance between the role sender and the focal persons are important topics in organizational behavior (Van sell, Brief, and Schuler).

Stress develops when an individual feels he is not competent to undertake the role assigned to him effectively. The individual feels that he lacks knowledge, skill and training on performing the role.

Miles and Perrault (1976) identify four different types of role conflict: 1. Intra-sender role conflict 2. Inter sender role conflict. 3. Person- role conflict; 4. Role over load. The use of role concepts suggests that work related stress is associated with individual, interpersonal, and structural variables (Katz and Kahn, 1978; Whitten, 1978). The presence of supportive peer groups and supportive relationships with super visors are negatively correlated with R.C. (Caplan et al., 1964).

Maslach (1978) looked at burnout as a "reaction to job related stress that results in the workers becoming emotionally detached clients, treating clients in dehumanizing ways, and becoming less effective on the job.

Marshal & Cooper in their study "work experience of middle and senior managers" (1979) looked at three managerial levels determine which job and organizational characteristics cause stress and satisfaction. They took in to consideration that it has long been assumed that higher level senior managers are most apt to experience job stress. The result revealed that middle managers showed more psychological and physical stress symptoms than senior managers as a result of the time pressure, responsibility, job problems with managing people, lack of autonomy and concern about career prospects. Senior Managers exhibited significantly lower amounts of job related stress and higher amount of job satisfaction. The authors suggested that organization concerned with managing executive stress should concentrate on middle level managers through efforts at job redesign, training, career development and organizational changes in order to reduce stress and increase productivity and performance.

Sampurna and Ansari (1979) Indian society is undergoing rapid social changes, such as, breakup of the joint family system and caste system, urbanization and rapid industrialization. These social changes have brought in their wake a number of stresses for the community at large. In this connection, studied the role of social factors in certain stress disorders-hypertension, peptic ulcers, thyrotoxicosis, bronchial asthma, anxiety neurosis etc. The social parameters used were family type, marital-status, education, economic status and urban/rural population. The results obtained prove conclusively that the joint family system gives rise to more stress disorders than intermediate and nuclear family. Moreover, incidence of such disorders was greater in higher educational categories and more hypersensitive came from the urban population.

Veninga&Spradley (1981) acknowledge that stress and burnout are complicated processes, and no easy solution is going to work for everyone. They write,

But we cannot reduce job burnout to a simple, uniform condition with a single personal treatment strategy. Consider these facts:

Unrelieved stress comes in packages of every conceivable shape and size. The risk factors can combine in a variety of ways to bring on job burnout. Each individual has a unique job-burnout threshold. Some people can take much larger doses of unrelieved stress than others before them burn out. The symptoms of burnout will vary from one person to the next. Each individual will learn to perceive stress in a unique way.

The severity of job burnout changes as it goes through each of the stages. Each individual will learn a different combination of stress safety valves to cope with job burnout and will need a unique combination to recover.

Maslach and Jackson (1981) have observed that burn out is a syndrome which includes emotional exhaustion and cynicism. Often, these are observed in individuals who are involved in people's work of the same type and results in the development of a negative cynical attitude and projected negative feelings towards the population to whom they are providing service.

Ivancevich, Matteson & Preston (1982) founded out that middle level managers experience more work stress on account of qualitative workload, lack of career progression, supervisor's relations and role conflict as compared to the lower and upper level managers.

Begley (1982) reported that their job pressures may result in a diminished job performance among administrators who are suffering from role conflict and burnout. Many times a climate of co-operation is obscured by conflict and stress between the individual and the organization. In many situations, such conflict and stress are precipitated from the internal desire of the individual administrator for professional autonomy and a license to exceed the perceived boundaries of the organization to provide for the needs of exceptional students.

Bishop (cited in Begley, 1982) indicated that burnout is not synonymous with the term 'stress". He pointed out that instead, burnout is a condition which is a side effect of stress, as well as other internal and external personal conflicts. Morocco and McFadden (1980) explained that organizational burnout can be defined as a collection of symptoms which are characterized by low morale in the workers, declining rates of overall production, elevated levels of work absenteeism, poor inadequate communication among the workers, and increased level of job attrition, when an organization is experiencing burnout, few organizational goals exist and the workers function with little sense of purpose.

Kobasa study 1982 has shown that hardly person develop fewer physical complaints under highly stressful condition than do person who are not hardly. Thus, hardiness may moderate the effects of the stress through the way people appraise and interpret those events in their lives.

❖ National Level:

Khan (1964) found in the study of men who suffered from role ambiguity, experience lower job satisfaction, higher job related tension and improper response about their achievements from the Management.

Gupta &Bech 1979 found in simple of vie companies, employees who experienced more of the job stressors of role ambiguity, role overload, under utilization of skills and resources inadequacy were somewhat more likely to be absents during the subsequent month than other employees furthermore, for three of the four stressors the correlation with the subsequent

35

absent was stronger than the correlation between these stressors and absenteeism prior to the measurement of the stressors. This comparison analysis was performed as a check on the potential confound that absenteeism was causing an increase in stressors rather than the other way around.

Further, **Madhur&Harigopal (1980)** who studied non-technical supervisors demonstrated that role ambiguity was negatively related to job involvement and performance.

Pastojee and Singh (1981) also used pareekh's ORS in a public utility enterprise and found a significant relationship between role stress and job satisfaction. They found focus of control as a mediating variable in their relationship.

In Study of officers of a private Organization, **Pastonjee& Singh (1982)** found that negatively associated with all dimensions of job Satisfaction, self role distance has significant negatively correlation with all the dimensions –job satisfaction and role inadequacy.

KiridaSurti (1982) studied the psychological correlates of role stress in working women in various professions. The eight different professional groups consisted of researchers, doctors, nurses, social workers, school teachers, university and college teachers, gazette officers and bank employees along with a group of forty women entrepreneurs. Analysis of scores revealed the typical stress experienced by a particular profession group and a rationale for this was sought. Self role distance was experienced mostly by bankers and least by university and college teachers. Doctors experience it to a very low extent. Role stagnation is experienced highest by nurses followed by bank employees and researchers.

D.M.Pestonjee studied 125 IAS officers in order to study role stress in government administration. The overall organizational stress for IAS officers was found to be 36.77% IAS officers scored high on inter role distance. This proves that they face greater conflicts among the various roles they occupy as officers and as a family man. The demands of the role are high and they find it difficult to form a correct balance between the different role they occupy, which creates stress and tension. They are unable to decide their priorities. The ISD officers scored high on self-role distance and their score was 4.5%. This situation would generally arise when there is mismatch between the job and the person. The role Ambiguity score is the lowest, which goes to prove that the IAS officers are very clear about the expectation of their roles.

Sen. (1982) in his study investigated the main role stresses experienced by employees in bank at different levels and the coping strategies adopted by them. He found that top level people had lower score on the stagnation whereas clerical staffs show the highest score on this dimension. The dimension of inter role distance has a lower rank among clerical staff, whereas it has a fairly high rank amongst top managers.

The background variables that Senstudied in relation to role stress were age, sex, education, income, family type, marital status, residence, distance from residence to place or work, distance from place of domicile to place of work. Entry and previous job experience. Some of the conclusion that Sen Draws are that role stagnation decreases as people advance in age – in general age is negatively related to role stress. Women experience more work stress as compared with men. Role stress is inversely related to income, the higher the income the lesser the role stress. Unmarried persons and persons with urban background experience more stress. Upbringing in rural areas may produce an attitude of self-contentment in contrast with the fast life activities of a city. The difficulties of commuting for people living 20-25 k.m away from place of work produce more stress than it does for people who live closer to the place of work. Family size was found to be positively related with role stagnation and role isolation and negatively with role erosion.

Jagdish and Srivastava (1983) studied the perceived stress and job satisfaction. The results show that employees' job satisfaction resulted in from on the job as well as off the job factors; it is significantly affected by their perceived role stress. A significant inverse relationship has been observed between the two variables.

Jagdish (1983) Studied the relationship between occupational stresses a job satisfaction . In his study arising out of role overload, role ambiguity, role conflict, group and political pressure, responsibility, under participation , powerlessness, poor relations intrinsic improvement, low status, hard working condition and non-profitability was found to have adverse effect of area wise as well as overall job satisfaction and negatively related with stress.

Srivastava and Sinha (1983) in their study found that subjects with high ego strength experienced mild stress arising from role overload, role ambiguity and role conflicts relative to that experienced by subjects with low or moderate ego strength. Similarly, subject with higher job involvement also experienced lower stress that those with low or moderate job involvement.

A Study was conducted by **Bharadwaj (1984)** on executives stress & its correlates, where it explored work stress and some related factors in 90 male public sectors managers-first, top and middle. The variables studies, related to work stress, the coping ability, the commitment of the workers and tend towards work holism. Result indicated that work stress is found at all managerial levels with different copping strategies. All managers show commitment to their organization though they are not workaholics.

Ahmed, Bharadwaj and Narula (1985) studied stress among the executives. They found the public and private sector executives did not differ in their role stress out of 10 dimension of role stress. However, significant differences were obtained on three viz. role isolation, role ambiguity and self role distance. It was observed that public sector executives have slightly more stress that their counterparts in the private sector. The background factors like age, education, income experience, marital status of the executives were found unrelated with their rile stress in both groups.

Srilata (1988) was of the opinion that among middle managers (both in public and private sectors) there was negative and significant correlation between role ambiguity and performance.

The High stress group perceives their job and work situation negatively and their subordinates and colleagues as low in work and a person orientation, than the low stress group. The low stress group is also more satisfied with their jobs, perceive their job as interesting having clarity are better acquainted with the job knowledge and have better rapport with their superior and subordinates.

Anoopsingh et al. (1991) rightly indicates that "Greater support from supervisors and co-workers in the workplace is strongly associated with greater feeling of well-being and any t undermining from their part put the employee under irritability, anxiety, depression, and somatic disorders. Inadequate support given by the superiors and their subordinates contribute considerable stress for employees in non-nationalized bank in this research.

OrganizeWork place Stress Management Programme that focuses on different leave categories of employees' at all hierarchical level. Many situational observations of employee & employer interaction identified within the organization can lead to stress at work these include.

- Relationships with co-workers.
- An unsupportive supervisor.

- Fear towards management.
- Lack of consultation and communication.
- Too much interference with employees' private, social or family life.
- Too much or too little to do
- Too much pressure, unrealistic deadlines
- Work that is too difficult or not demanding enough
- Lack of control over the way the work is done
- Poor working conditions
- Being in the wrong job
- Feeling undervalued
- Feeling Job difficulty
- Insecurity and the threat of unemployment.

Another study was conducted by **Desai (1994)** in the industrial organization —"Stress and mental workload". This study attempted to identify and determine the different response profile of the levels of the management. The result indicated that higher and middle level of management had higher levels of stress and mental workload, followed by lower stress.

CHAPTER-III
RESEARCH METHODOLOGY

- ## Title:

"A Study on Employee work place Stress". A study undertaken of Middle level Employees of Sabar Dairy, Himatnagar.

- ## Significance of the study:

Employee work place stress is the growing factor, which have effected & influenced the individual behavior in the organization and this factor is seen clearly because of influence of the multinational organization, changing government, economics policies, globalization etc.

The ladder of success built upon the ropes of stress as human beings are involved in the neck-to-neck competition to reach the zenith. Work place stress is a process by which the organization becomes deformed slowly and gradually by the constant impairment of the system stress can be productive and stimulate creativity and enthusiasm leading to better and more imaginative. Performance but prolonged and high-level of stress can have negative effects.

Today the organizational function in a very dynamic environment and have to face the challenges of competition. This brings into picture many issues related to work performance, work moral and organizational growth. It is thus imperative for managers to remain effective in such competitive environment.

Meeting the rising customer's expectation knowledge and information. Explosion and the technological advancements are some of the challenges for the manager it creates a stressful environment for the managers to consistently delivers their best. However, the HR function here is to understand the psychological part of work related stress and develop strategies to cope up with the same.

The present study is primarily intended to understand the work place stress level in private Organizations. It is significant since it has a potential to generate data and subsequently useful information in areas of Work Place Stress.

- **Objective of the study:**
  - To Study the level of stress faced by the middle level employees in Sabar dairy.
  - To study types of 'work stress' faced by the middle level employees in Sabar dairy.
  - To study internal and external work stress during work of employees in Sabar dairy.
  - To give suggestion to reduce the amount of work stress handle by employees to the management of Sabar dairy.

- **Universe:**
The Universe of the study is 1039 Middle level employees in Sabar Dairy, Himatnagar.

- **Sample & Sampling Method:**
Random Sampling method was used to select the respondents from the whole universe to collect information of

50 respondents, the sample consist of middle level management employees working in various department.

- **Research Design:**
  The study is exploratory in nature in which it explores the work place stress.

- **Variables:**
- **Dependent variable:**
  ➢ Work Place Stress

- **Independent Variables:**
  ➢ Age
  ➢ Gender (Sex)
  ➢ Educational Qualification
  ➢ Income per- month
  ➢ Work Experience

- **Operational Definitions:**
  - **Workplace Stress:**
  Workplace stress is the harmful physical and emotional response that occurs when there is a poor match between job demands and the capabilities, resources, or needs of the worker. Stress-related disorders encompass a broad array of conditions, including psychological disorders (e.g., depression, anxiety, post-traumatic stress disorder) and other types of emotional strain (e.g., dissatisfaction, fatigue, tension, etc.), maladaptive behaviors (e.g., aggression, substance abuse), and cognitive impairment (e.g., concentration and memory problems). In turn,

these conditions may lead to poor work performance or even injury. Job stress is also associated with various biological reactions that may lead ultimately to compromised health, such as cardiovascular disease.

- **Tool for Data Collection:**

    A structured questionnaire was used as a tool for data collection, which consist of closed ended questions.

- **Analysis of data:**

    The data was analyzedby frequency distribution and percentage method and presentedin the form of simple Tables & Column –charts.

- **Limitation of the study:**
- A time factor was considered as a limitation as one has to complete at a specific time.
- The study on work place stress has considered as a drop in the ocean of stress.

- **Chapteriation:**

Chapter-I: Introduction

    It covers various aspects of Work place stress.

Chapter-II: Review of Literature

    It covers the review of researcher based on empirical data as well as articles based on the observational evidence of the authorized journals.

Chapter-III: Research Methodology

It covers the significance of the study, objectives, universe, sample & sampling method, tolls of data collection, limitation of the study, Variables etc.

Chapter-IV: Research Setting:

It covers the background information of the organization form where the data is collected.

Chapter-V: Data Analysis:

This chapter covers the data in the analyze form & also interpretations of each kind of data.

Chapter-VI: Findings, Conclusion, suggestions & plan of action:

It covers major finding from the interpretation of the data, Conclusion, suggestion & plan of action for to reduce Work place Stress among the middle level employee.

Sabarkantha District Co-operative
Milk Producer's Union Ltd.Himatnagar

- **BACKGROUND OF DAIRY**

The Sabarkantha District Co-operative Milk Producers Union Limited, Himatnagaris also known as Sabar Dairy. The main objective of Sabar Dairy is to collect milk from Sabarkantha District and manufacture different types of milk product for customers at lowest price. The milk products manufactured by Sabar Dairy are marketed by GCMMF (Gujarat Cooperative Milk Marketing Federation), Anand under the brand name of 'Amul'. In short, all major activities related to marketing are done on the priority of the GCMMF.

Sabar Dairy was established in 1964 and got its name as it is situated in Sabarkantha   District. First time milk was collected in 1964 on 29th September, 1965. It has also got certificate ISO 9001:2008 for quality, ISO 14000 for environment and ISO-22000 for quality and food safety purpose.

The great SardarVallabhbhai Patel suggests establishing co-operative dairy and with his suggestion, first Amul Dairy and then Sabar Dairy were established. Under the direction of Bhurabhai k. Patel the milk production was promoted in the Sabarkantha District in 1964. In 1971, NDDB introduced a program called "operation flood" which provided finance for developing plant. The civil construction and plant design were executed by NDDB.

Saber dairy has mainly seven departments:

- Production department
- Marketing department
- Finance department
- Human Resource department
- Milk procurement
- Animal Husbandry department
- Quality Assurance

These all seven departments are working efficiently. The Milk Procurement department has their main activity to collect milk, check it and produce different milk base products. The marketing departments do their job under GCMMF. The finance department has main duty to utilize scare resources efficiently an also manage the resources. The HR department has to perform activities like to give training to new person, selection, recruitment, promotion and so many others.

The dairy is divided in three major parts:

- Administrative building
- Veterinary building
- Factory unit

- **DAIRY PROFILE AND OTHER INFORMATION**

1) NAME OF THE DAIRY:

Sabarkantha District Co-operative Milk Producers Union Ltd.

2) ADDRESS:
Sabar Dairy
Sub post: Boria,
Himatnagar.
Gujarat – 383006

3) PHONE:
02772-226051 to 60

4) FAX No:
02772-226130

5) E-MAIL ADDRESS:
amul@sabardairy.coop.

6) WEB SITE:
www.**sabardairy**.org

7) CORPORATE ADDRESS:
Gujarat cooperative milk marketing federation ltd.
Anand, Gujarat.

8) CHAIRMAN:
Shri JethabhaiPrabhudas Patel

9) VICE CHAIRMAN:
Shri JayantibhaiBhikhabhai Patel

10) MANAGING DIRECTOR:
Dr. B.M.Patel

11) Auditor:
Special audit (milk),

Milk audit office, Himatnagar.

12) Bankers:
The Sabarkantha District Co-operative Bank

State Bank of India (Himatnagar)

Bank of Baroda(Himatnagar) and

Dena Bank(Himatnagar)

13) Licence:
Saber Dairy was registered with the name of Sabarkantha District Co-operative Milk Producer's Union Ltd. in Gujarat.

14) Apex decision:
GCMMF, Anand, Gujarat.

15) FORM OF DAIRY
Sabar Dairy can be classified as a large scale dairy industry.
16) LIST OF BOARD OF DIRECTOR
1. Shri KhemabhaiHirabhai Patel
2. Shri JasubhaiShivubhai Patel
3. Shri RambhaiJivabhai Patel
4. Shri BhogilalRamanbhai Patel
5. Shri KantibhaiSomabhai Patel
6. Shri DhulabhaiKodarbhai Patel
7. Shri SubhasbhaiNathabhai Patel
8. Shri JeshingbhaiRambhai Patel
9. Shri VipulbhaiRambhai Patel
10. Shri LilachandbhaiBahechardas Patel
11. Shri DaulatsinghJagatsingh Chauhan

12. Shri ManibhaiIshwarbhai Patel
13. Shri JayantibhaiVirchandbhai Patel
14. Shri KantibhaiDhulabhai Patel

17) AWARDS:

The company has achieved the following national level awards during different years.

1) 1987/88 :- The National productivity awards
2) 1989/90 :- The National productivity awards
3) 1999/00:- The National productivity awards
4) 1997/98 :- The National awards
5) 2000/01 :- The Gujarat safety awards
6) 2008/09 :- Kaizen Kingdom award
7) 2002/03 :- The National productivity awards
8) 2005/06 :-   The National productivity awards
9) 2005:- Minimum Safety council awards
10) 2006:- Minimum Safety council awards

- **VISION AND MISSION OF THE COMPANY**
➢ **Vision and mission:**
1) Being global leader especially for indigenous products.

2)   Also more concentration on no. of products and quality of products.

3) Lifting BPL, that is who come under BPL (below poverty line) by giving direct loan or grant to them and also by providing animals.

➢ Objectives:

1) To provide a better quality milk at lower price.

2) Try to make optimum veterans to its member and share holder.

3) To assist in development of small village and try to co-operate them.

4) To minimize the adverse effect on the environment.

5) To maintain better relationship to their member.

6) To provide zero defects products.

7) Acceptance of international standards for food safety.

▪ ORGANIZATION

Saber Dairy is a Milk Producers' Co-operative Union working for the socio-economic welfare of milk producers of Sabarkantha district of Gujarat in India. It is the largest industry in Sabarkantha. It instills the self-confidence and self-respect to the rural milk producers. It is the lifeline of Sabarkantha district. It packs pure milk and produces milk products under the brand Amul. It is one of the largest milk producers' co-operative unions in India. It aims to provide remunerative returns to the farmers (milk producers) and serve the interest of consumers by providing quality milk products throughout India and abroad by a network of dealers through its Federation, M/s Gujarat Co-operative Milk Marketing Federation Limited, headquartered at Anand. Sabar Union procures milk from its 1780 member co-operative societies twice a day round the year. It packs liquid milk and produces almost all types of milk products. The major products it produces include Butter, Infant milk powder, dairy whitener, Ghee, Paneer, Curd (Dahi) & Buttermilk etc. all under Amul brand. It operates as a three-tiered structure starting from Village Milk Cooperative Society-District Milk Producers' Union-Federation of District Unions at the State level.

- **TYPES OF COMMUNICATION CHANNEL**

There are mainly two types of communication:

1. Internal communication
2. External communication

Internal communication can be done by telephone, mobile phone, circulars, reports, regular   meetings etc. Regular meeting is arranged on every Thursday in each department. Similarly monthly and annually general meetings are also arranged.

External communication is placed by responsible person, federation etc. There is no   media communication in Saber Dairy.

- **PRESENT MANPOWER STATUS**

There are 1039 employees in Saber Dairy.

- Managerial : 40
- Officer : 160
- Clerical : 464
- Unskilled : 375

- **PRESENT PRODUCT MIX**
  - Amul spray powder
  - Amul butter
  - Amul instant milk food(Amulya)
  - Amul ghee
  - AmulMastiDahi
  - Amul Kool
  - Amul paneer
  - Amulsrikhand
  - Amul milk(shakti, gold, shathi)
  - Amul butter milk
  - Amulskimed milk

- **FUTURE EXPANSION PLAN**
  - Establishing new milk processing plant of 12 lakh litre.
  - Introducing new dairy marketing in North India
  - Establishing energy saving plant
  - Establishing automatic manufacturing plant for Paneer.
  - Try to make Automation and Computerization system.

- **STRATEGIES OR FUTURE GROWTH AND DEVELOPMENT**

  Being global leader is one of the main aim or vision of Saber Dairy. Initially there was no competitor. But this is not the case presently. Nowadays there are so many competitors like nestle, Cadbury, Glexo, loose market of milk, Royal Dairy and so many others which are able to be global leader.

For growing more and more Saber Dairy tries to be aware more and more about consumer. Satisfaction of customer needs is to be considered mostly. Other strategy is introducing new and qualitative products. Providing loan or grants and also other benefits to workers and employees is also there in Saber Dairy for growing employees status and satisfaction and bring them over BPL (below poverty line).

Saber Dairy should plan its strategies in such a way that they prove to be beneficial to the   organization as a whole. The main strategies of Saber Dairy are as follows:

- Good quality product
- Innovation
- Timely deliveries
- Better design of the products
- Reasonable price
- Relationship building
- Response to dealers on time
- Customer care
- Timely payment to their customers

- **POLICIES USED BY SABAR DAIRY**

There are mainly three types of policies used by Saber Dairy:

- Quality and Food Safety Policy
- Animal infertility eradication policy
- Animal feeding and breeding management policy

1. Quality policy:-

We at Saber Dairy are commited to continuously

Strive......

To manufacture and supply and quality and safe milk and milk product

To.......

Eliminate the risk of consumer health

To uplift the socioeconomic status of members, producers and employees

To satisfy needs and expectation of the consumers.

By........

Complying with all applicable statutory, regulatory and other requirements, continuous improvement of quality and food safety management system. By upgrading of Technology efficient utilization of available resources, providing require resources, achieving set objectives within time frame, efficient communication at all levels and review this policy regularly.

To ....

Be a global leader in the field of dairy industries.

2.Animal infertility eradication policy:-
Sabar Dairy is determined to eradicate infertility amongst milk animals from Sabarkantha District.

3. Feeding and breeding management policy:-

Sabar dairy continuously endeavors to improve breeding efficiency and milk productivity in milky animals.

- **SWOT ANALYSIS**
STRENGTH OF COMPANY:-

1. Labor availability:
Saber dairy is situated on national highway no.8, just 5 k.m. away from Himatnagar- the district head quarter. This makes easy availability of labors.

2. Low transportation cost:
The location is the center of sabarkantha district, so it gets milk from whole sabarkantha district easily and in time with low transportation cost.

3. Competitive staff:
Whole technical staff of the company is well educated and competitive. These people have vast experience in the milk industry.

4. Financial strong:
Saber Dairy is built in backward area, so it is getting some financial aids from government. N.D.D.B. has granted loan of RS. 8,91,96,938 under operation flood-2 and 9,86,26,462 under operation flood-3.

WEAKNESS OF COMPANY:-

1. Centralization of the authority:
In Saber dairy all decisions and actions plans flow only from chairman's end. Most apex decisions are taken by the GCMMF.

2. Liberal management:
There is some possibility that, chairman is not competent to take major decisions. Chairman is elected by directors, so there are some politics also prevailing.

OPPORTUNITY OF COMPANY:-

1. Globalization:
The company has to become "A Global leader in the field of dairy industry". So, there is tremendous opportunity to capture the global market around the world. So this proves to be an opportunity for the company to increase the revenue.

2. Distribution by local agent:
Saber dairy is concerned with the GCMMF through which whole marketing is done. So it has no local agents. So they have an opportunity to expand their distribution channel by covering local agents also.

THREAT OF COMPANY:-
1. Political interference:
Major decisions are taken by the elected chairman and there are some political pressure prevailing on the taken decisions, so it becomes the threat for the company.

2. Globalization:
Globalization along with some benefits it has adverse effects also, because it gives birth to the competition which is the big threat for the company.

3. Natural calamities:
Due to that there is a shortage of resources, it break down the continuous activity of milk procurement process.

CHAPTER-V
DATA ANALYSIS

Table.1 Showing the age of the respondents.

Sr. no	Age	Frequency	Percentage
1	18 to 25 years	15	30
2	26 to 30 years	20	40
3	31 to 40 years	10	20
4	41 & more	5	10
	Total	**50**	**100**

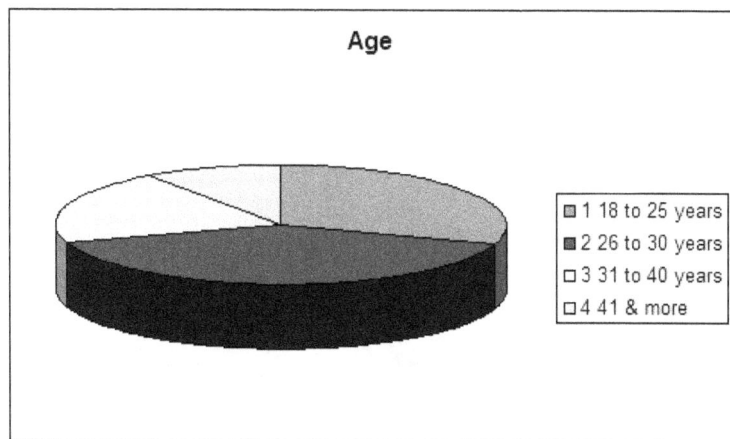

Interpretation:

From above the table it can be analyzed that majority 20 (40 Percentage) respondents are between the ages of 26 to 30 years, when 15 (30 Percentage) respondents are the age of 18 to 25 years, and 10 (20 Percentage) respondents are between the age of 31 to 40 years of age, while only 5(10 Percentage) respondents are between the age of 41 & more years. So from the Table it can be analyzed that the majority respondents are from the middle age.

Table.2 Showing the Gender of the respondents.

Sr. no	Gender	Frequency	Percentage
1	Male	40	80
2	Female	10	20
	Total	**50**	**100**

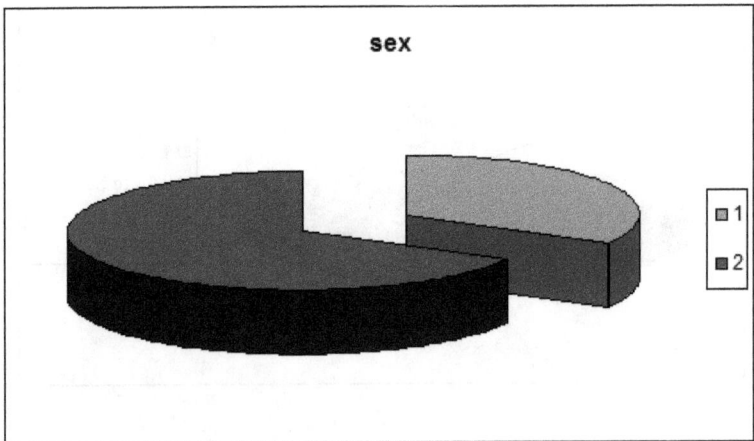

Interpretation:

From above given table it can be Conclude that majority 40 (80Percentage) respondents are the males, while only 10(20 Percentage) respondents are female.

Table.3 Showing the Educational qualification of the respondents.

Sr. no	Educational Qualification	Frequency	Percentage
1	S.S.C	10	20
2	H.S.C	12	24
3	Graduate	24	48
4	Post graduate	4	8
	Total	**50**	**100**

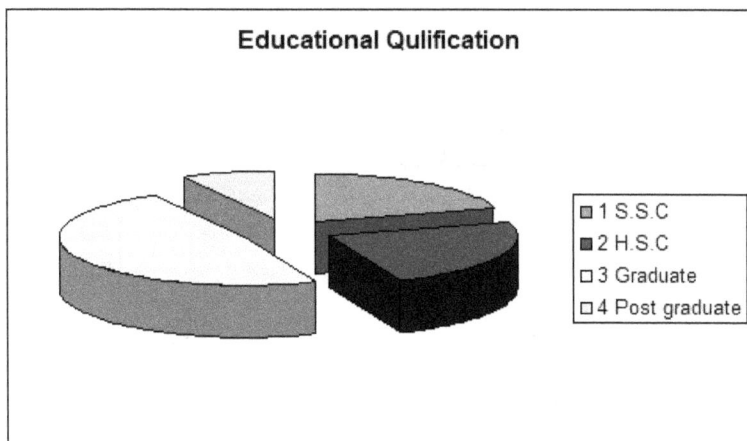

Educational Qulification

□ 1 S.S.C
■ 2 H.S.C
□ 3 Graduate
□ 4 Post graduate

Interpretation:

From above given table it can be analyzed that majority 24(48 Percentage) respondents are graduate, while 12 (24 Percentage) respondents are only H.S.C passed, & 10(20 Percentage) respondents are only 10th passed, while 4 (8 Percentage) respondents are Post graduate.

Table.4 Showing the income/month of the respondents.

Sr. no	Income/month	Frequency	Percentage
1	8000 to 12000	10	20
2	12000 to 16000	10	20
3	16000 to 20000	20	40
4	20000 & more	10	20
	Total	**50**	**100**

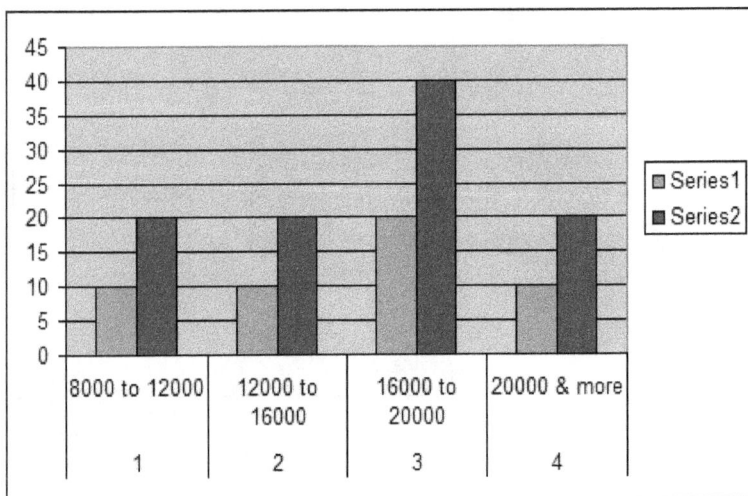

Interpretation:

From above given table it can be analyzed that majority, 20 (40 Percentage) respondents are getting 16000 to 20000 Rs/month, while 10 (20 Percentage) respondents are getting 12000 to 16000 Rs/month, but 10 (20 Percentage) respondents are getting only 8000 to 12000 Rs/month, and only 10 (20 Percentage) respondents are getting 20000& more Rs/month.

Table.5 Showing the experience of the respondents

Sr. no	Work Experience	Frequency	Percentage
1	0 - 2 year	20	40
2	2- 4 year	15	30
3	4-7 year	6	12
4	7-10 year	5	10
5	10 year	4	8
	Total	50	100

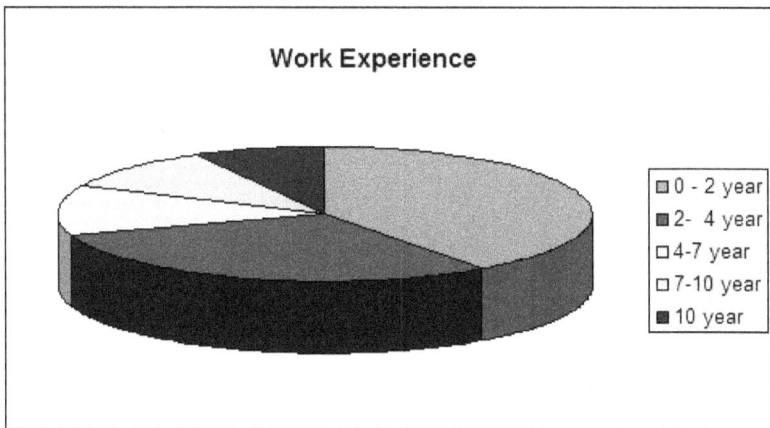

Work Experience

- 0 - 2 year
- 2- 4 year
- 4-7 year
- 7-10 year
- 10 year

Interpretation:

From above the table it can be analyzed that Majority 20(40 Percentage) respondents have 0 to 2 years of experience, while 15 (30 Percentage) respondents have 2 to 4 years of experience, and 6 (12Percentage) respondents have 4 to7 years of experience, and 5 (10 percentage) 7 to 10 years of experience, but only 4(8 Percentage) respondents have 10 years of experience.

Table.6 Showing the response of the respondents whether they feel physically or emotionally   tedious.

Sr. NO	Particular	No of Respondents	Percentage of respondents
1	Not at all	2	4
2	Rarely	25	50
3	Sometime	23	46
4	Often	0	0
5	Very Often	0	0
	Total	50	100

feel rundown and drained of physical or emotional energy at work

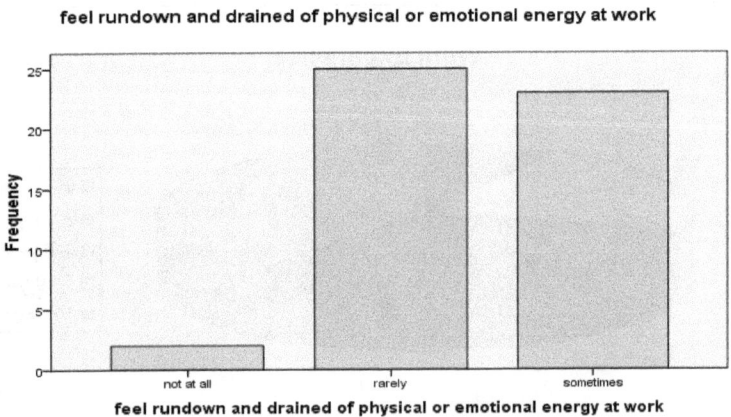

feel rundown and drained of physical or emotional energy at work

Interpretation:

From above the table it can be analyzed that majority of the Respondents feel the physical or emotional energy-level normal, the percentage of the rarely is 25 (50 Percentage), while only 23 (46 Percentage) respondents feel the tedium sometimes. And only 2(4 percentage) respondents feel no tedium at the work place.

Thus majority of the respondents face the wearisome state to some rare occasions.

Table.7 Showing the response of the respondents whether they face negative waves at work Place or not.

Sr. NO	Particular	No of Respondents	Percentage of respondents
1	Not at all	42	84
2	Rarely	4	8
3	Sometime	4	8
4	Often	0	0
5	Very Often	0	0
	Total	50	100

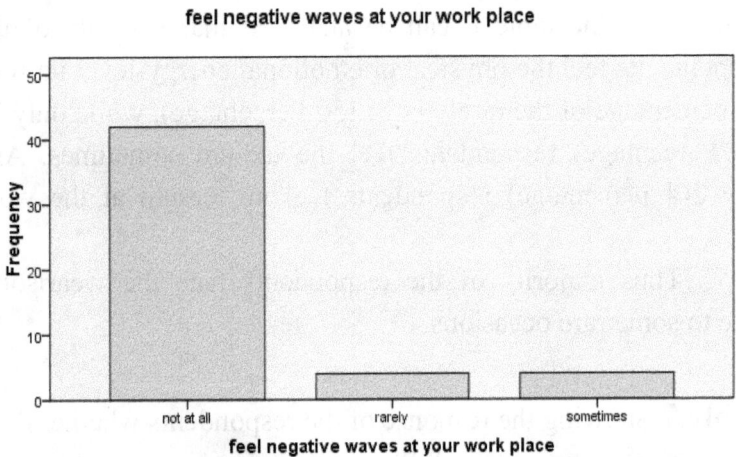

feel negative waves at your work place

Interpretation:

From above the table it can be analyzed that majority of the Respondents that is 42(84 percentage) feel the negative waves not at all, the percentage of the rarely is 4 (8 Percentage), while only 4 (8 Percentage) respondents feel the negative waves sometimes. And only 4(8 percentage) respondents face them sometimes at the work place.

Thus majority of the respondents face them never.

Table.8 Showing the response of the respondents whether they face the problem of being Unappreciated by co-workers or Supervisor.

Sr. NO	Particular	No of Respondents	Percentage of respondents
1	Not at all	29	59
2	Rarely	21	41
3	Sometime	0	0

4	Often	0	0
5	Very Often	0	0
	Total	50	100

you are misunderstood or unappreciated by your co-workers and supervisor

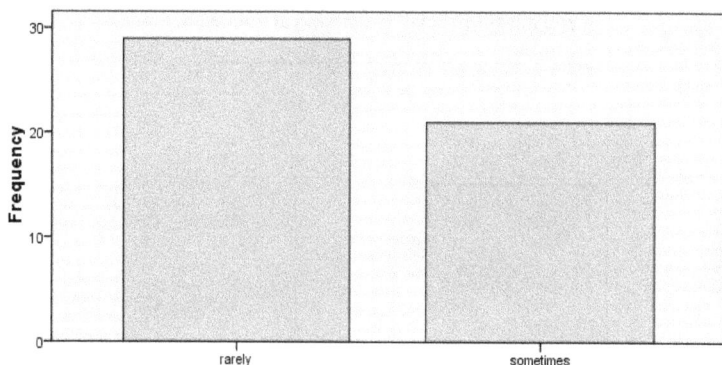

you are misunderstood or unappreciated by your co-workers and supervisor

Interpretation:

From above the table it can be analyzed that majority of the Respondents that is 29(59 percentage) feel never to be misunderstood or unappreciated, and only 21 (41 Percentage), of the employee seldom feel such state.

Thus majority of the respondents face them never.

Table.9 Showing the response of the respondents whether they feel lack of the   social Networking sites at the work place.

Sr. NO	Particular	No of Respondents	Percentage of respondents
1	Not at all	21	41
2	Rarely	29	59

3	Sometime	0	0
4	Often	0	0
5	Very Often	0	0
	Total	50	100

are you missing social networking at your work place

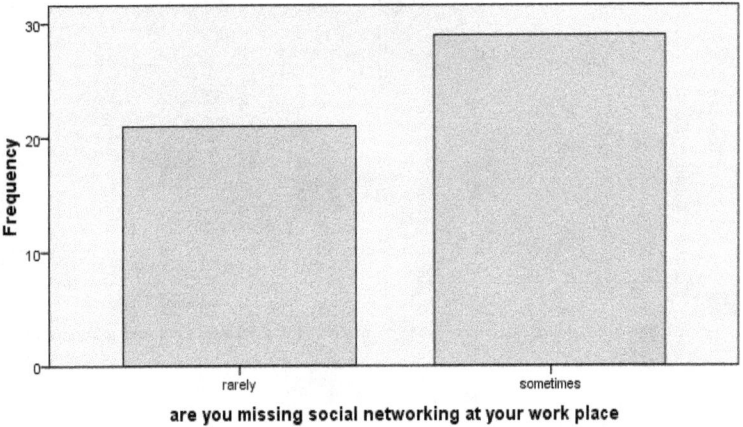

are you missing social networking at your work place

Interpretation:

From above the table it can be analyzed that majority of the Respondents that is 29 (59 percentage) miss the social networking web rarely, the percentage of feeling not at all is 21(41 Percentage).

Thus majority of the respondents feel the lack rarely.

Table.10

Showing the response of the respondents whether they feel the state of Dissatisfaction in terms of their chievements.

Sr. NO	Particular	No of Respondents	Percentage of respondents
1	Not at all	33	63
2	Rarely	14	28
3	Sometime	3	6
4	Often	0	0
5	Very Often	0	0
	Total	50	100

do you feel that you have achieved is less then your capacity due to stress

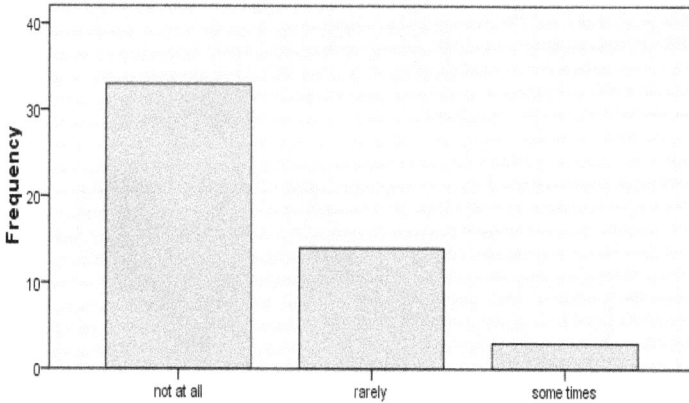

do you feel that you have achieved is less then your capacity due to stress

Interpretation:

The table shows that From above the table it can be analyzed that majority of the Respondents that is 33(63 percentage) feel such dissatisfaction not at all, the percentage of the rarely is14 (28 Percentage), while only 3 (6 Percentage) respondents feel such state sometimes.

Thus majority of the respondents feel such state never.

Table.11 Showing the response of the respondents whether they feel the level of
Pressure at the work place to be got work done.

Sr. NO	Particular	No of Respondents	Percentage of respondents
1	Not at all	7	14
2	Rarely	28	56
3	Sometime	15	30
4	Often	0	0
5	Very Often	0	0
	Total	50	100

do you feel an unpleasant level of pressure at your work to get work done

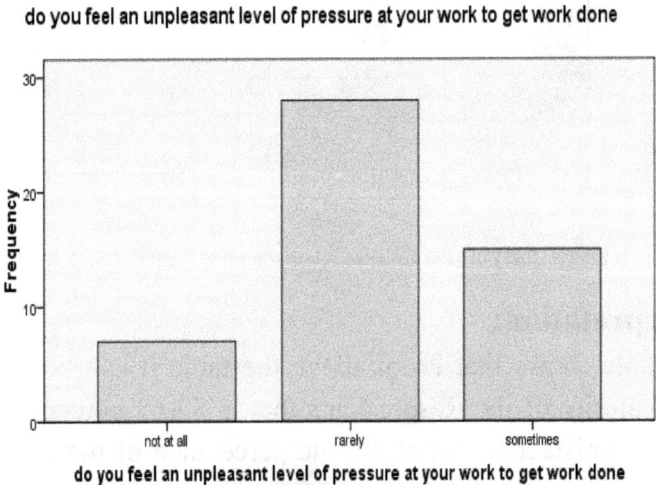

do you feel an unpleasant level of pressure at your work to get work done

Interpretation:

From above the table it can be analyzed that majority of the Respondents that is 28(56 percentage) feel the working pressure rarely. , the percentage of the employee feeling it sometimes is 15 (30 Percentage), while only 7 (14 Percentage) respondents feel it never.

Thus majority of the respondents face them rarely.

Table.12 Showing the response of the respondents whether the job being allotted to the employee is of his/her interest.

Sr. NO	Particular	No of Respondents	Percentage of respondents
1	Not at all	0	0
2	Rarely	28	56
3	Sometime	22	44
4	Often	0	0
5	Very Often	0	0
	Total	50	100

the job has been given to you is not of your area of interest

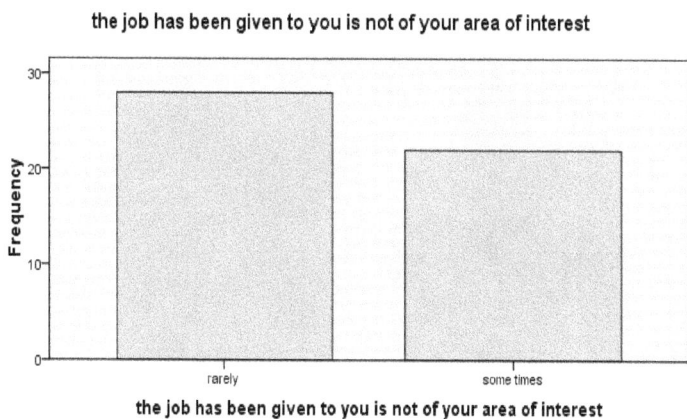

the job has been given to you is not of your area of interest

Interpretation:

From above the table it can be analyzed that majority of the Respondents that is 28(56 percentage) rarely feel the job uninteresting, the percentage feeling it sometimes is 22(44 Percentage).

Thus majority of the respondents feels the job uninteresting rarely.

Table.13 Showing the response of the respondents whether they face problem due to workload in their personal development.

Sr. NO	Particular	No of Respondents	Percentage of respondents
1	Not at all	0	0
2	Rarely	15	30
3	Sometime	20	40
4	Often	15	30
5	Very Often	0	0
	Total	50	100

due to heavy load of work you haven't extra time to spend for personal development

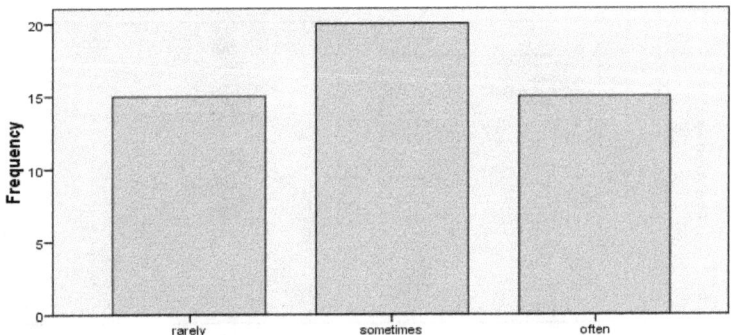

due to heavy load of work you haven't extra time to spend for personal development

Interpretation:

    From above the table it can be analyzed that majority of the Respondents that is 20(40 percentage) feel such obstacle sometimes, the percentage of being felt so rarely is 15 (30 Percentage), while only 15 (30 Percentage) respondents often feel such obstacle.

Thus majority of the respondents face it sometimes.

Table.14 Showing the response of the respondents whether they feel the shortage of time because of the heavy load of work.

Sr. NO	Particular	No of Respondents	Percentage of respondents
1	Not at all	0	0
2	Rarely	22	44
3	Sometime	10	20
4	Often	18	36
5	Very Often	0	0
	Total	50	100

do you feel heavy load of your work at time you maintain quality of your job

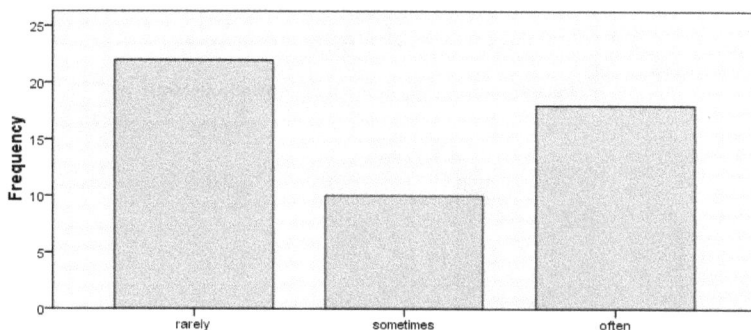

do you feel heavy load of your work at time you maintain quality of your job

Interpretation:

From above the table it can be analyzed that majority of the Respondents that is 22(44 percentage) feel such problem rarely, the percentage of facing such problem often is 18 (36 Percentage), while only 10 (20 Percentage) respondents feel the problem sometimes.

Thus majority of the respondents face this problem rarely.

Table.15 Showing the response of the respondents whether they feel frustration/tension due to non-achievement of their target.

Sr. NO	Particular	No of Respondents	Percentage of respondents
1	Not at all	0	0
2	Rarely	22	44
3	Sometime	23	46
4	Often	5	10
5	Very Often	0	0
	Total	50	100

get frustration/tension for non-achievement of your target

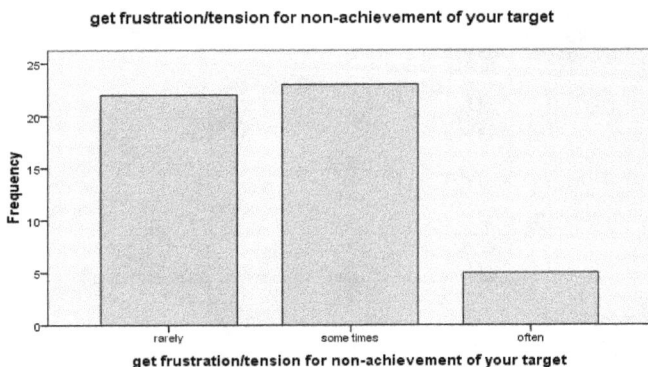

get frustration/tension for non-achievement of your target

Interpretation:

From above the table it can be analyzed that majority of the Respondents that is 23(46 percentage) feel such sort of tension sometimes, the percentage of feeling it rarely is 22 (44 Percentage), while only 5 (10 Percentage) respondents often feel it .Thus majority of the respondents face such tension some times.

Table.16 Showing the response of the respondents whether they face the problem of rageof theirboss and supervisor due to poor performance.

Sr. NO	Particular	No of Respondents	Percentage of respondents
1	Not at all	1	2
2	Rarely	29	58
3	Sometime	18	36
4	Often	2	4
5	Very Often	0	0
	Total	50	100

supervisor or boss sought on you due to poor performance

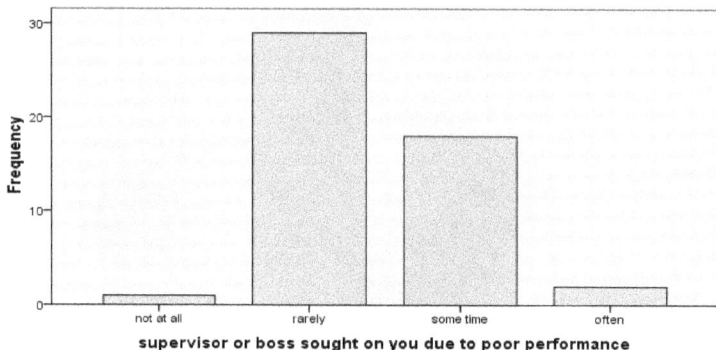

supervisor or boss sought on you due to poor performance

Interpretation:

From above the table it can be analyzed that majority of the Respondents that is 29(58 percentage) is being souted by their dignitaries rarely, while 18 (36 Percentage) respondents face such scolding some times. And only 2(4 percentage) respondents face it often at the work place.

Thus majority of the respondents rarely face such problem.

Table.17 Showing the response of the respondents whether their work load forces them to work beyond working hours.

Sr. NO	Particular	No of Respondents	Percentage of respondents
1	Not at all	0	0
2	Rarely	39	78
3	Sometime	11	22
4	Often	0	0
5	Very Often	0	0
	Total	50	100

your work load force you to work beyond working hours

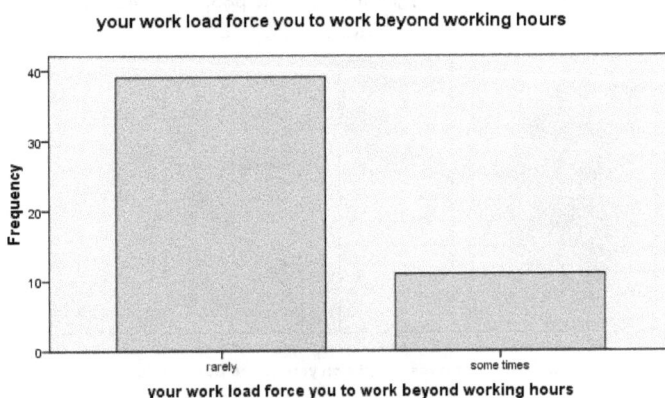

your work load force you to work beyond working hours

Interpretation:

From above the table it can be analyzed that majority of the Respondents that is 39(78 percentage) rarely face such problem, 11 (22 Percentage)of the respondents face sometimes such problems at the work place.

Thus majority of the respondents face this problem rarely.

Table.18 Showing the response of the respondents whether they take support of entertainment to kill work stress.

Sr. NO	Particular	No of Respondents	Percentage of respondents
1	Not at all	0	0
2	Rarely	0	0
3	Sometime	4	8
4	Often	25	50
5	Very Often	21	42
	Total	50	100

you take support of entertainment to kill work stress

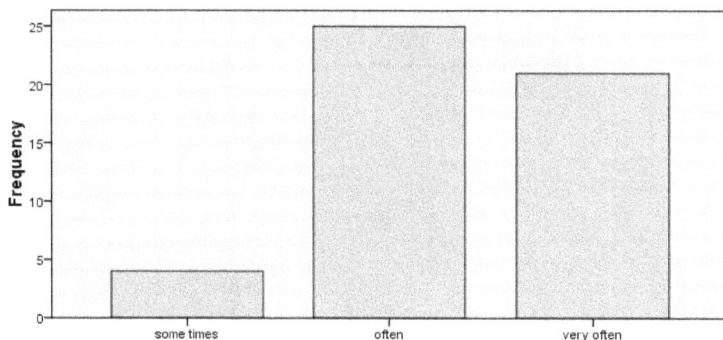

you take support of entertainment to kill work stress

Interpretation:

From above the table it can be analyzed that majority of the Respondents that is 25(50 percentage) often takes such kind of diversion, whereas 21 (42 Percentage) respondents very often take this. And only 4(8 percentage) respondents some time take such diversion.

Thus majority of the respondents often take this sort of refreshment.

Table.19 Showing the response of the respondents whether they get to have balance between work life and social life.

Sr. NO	Particular	No of Respondents	Percentage of respondents
1	Not at all	1	2
2	Rarely	0	0
3	Sometime	32	64
4	Often	17	34
5	Very Often	0	0
	Total	50	100

balance between work life and social life

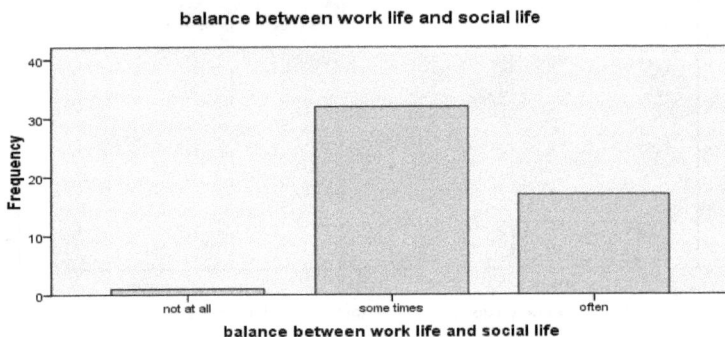

balance between work life and social life

Interpretation:

From above the table it can be analyzed that majority of the Respondents that is 32(64 percentage) sometimes manages to keep such balance between these two, while 17 (34 Percentage) respondents often manage to do so. And only 1(2 percentage) respondents fail to do so.

Thus majority of the respondents sometimes manage to maintain such balance.

Table.20 Showing the response of the respondents whether they feel fear of accident/hazards associated with their work place.

Sr NO	Particular	No of Respondents	Percentage of respondents
1	Not at all	41	82
2	Rarely	9	18
3	Sometime	0	0
4	Often	0	0
5	Very Often	0	0
	Total	50	100

accident/hazards associated with your work place

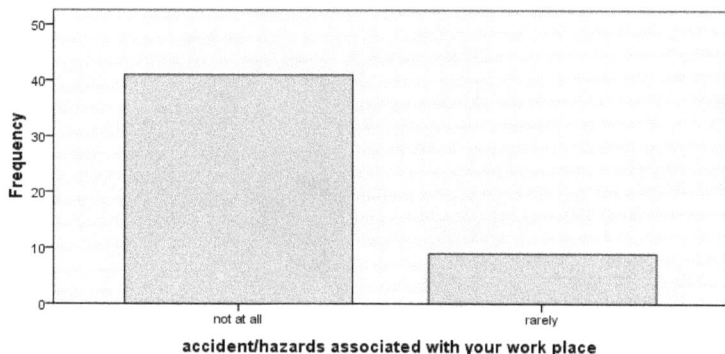

accident/hazards associated with your work place

Interpretation:

From above the table it can be analyzed that majority of the Respondents that is 41(82 percentage) never feels this kind of fear, while 9 (18 Percentage) respondents rarely feel this kind of fear.

Thus majority of the respondents never feel such sort of fear.

Table.21 Showing the response of the respondents whether their job allow them to attain each social function.

Sr. NO	Particular	No of Respondents	Percentage of respondents
1	Not at all	0	0
2	Rarely	2	4
3	Sometime	20	40
4	Often	16	32
5	Very Often	12	24
	Total	50	100

your job allow you to attain each social function

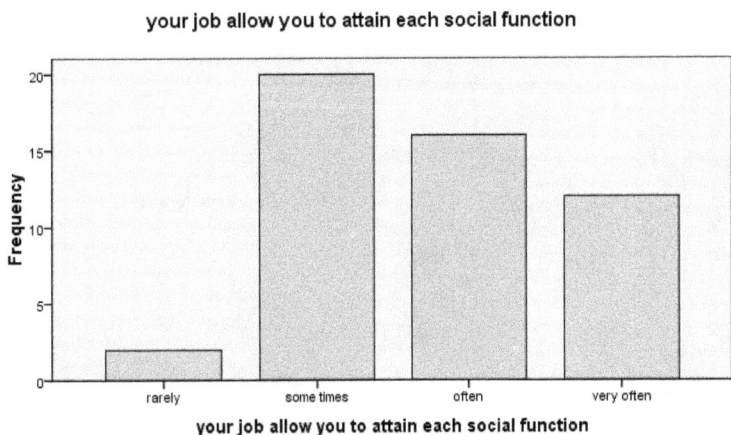

your job allow you to attain each social function

Interpretation:

From above the table it can be analyzed that majority of the Respondents that is 20(40 percentages) sometimes feels ease to attain each social function. While 16 (32 Percentage) respondents often feel comfortable to tackle the both. And only 12(24 percentage) respondents very often make it attainable, while just 2(4 percentage) rarely manage to do so.

Thus majority of the respondents sometimes finds it easy to attain it social function along with their job.

Table.22 Showing the response of the respondents whether they find themselves getting easily irritate by small problems, or by their Co-workers and team.

Sr. NO	Particular	No of Respondents	Percentage of respondents
1	Not at all	29	58
2	Rarely	9	18
3	Sometime	6	12
4	Often	2	4
5	Very Often	4	8
	Total	50	100

are you easily irritate small problems co-workers and team

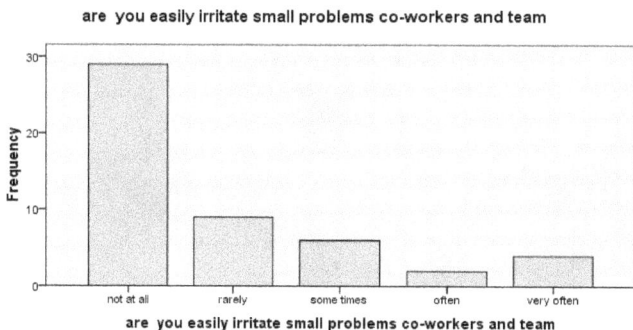

are you easily irritate small problems co-workers and team

Interpretation:

From above the table it can be analyzed that majority of the Respondents that is 29(58 percentage) doesn't feel irritated by small problems or by collegues. While 9(18 Percentage) respondents rarely find it easy to tackle. And only 6(12 percentage) respondents sometimes get irritated due to small blunders, while just 4(8 percentage) very often get irritated in such problems, and only 2(4 percentage) often get furiated in such situation.

Thus majority of the respondents never lose their temperament.

Table.23 Showing the response of the respondents whether they are very clear about their responsibilities, roles, activities associated with your job.

Sr. NO	Particular	No of Respondents	Percentage of respondents
1	Not at all	0	0
2	Rarely	4	8
3	Sometime	18	36
4	Often	17	34
5	Very Often	11	22
	Total	50	100

you are much clear about your responsibilities,roles,activities,priorities associated your job

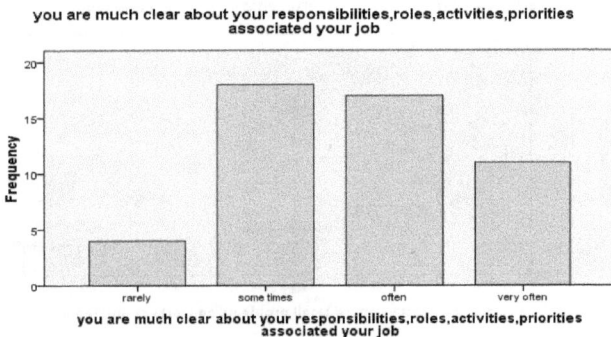

you are much clear about your responsibilities,roles,activities,priorities associated your job

Interpretation:

From above the table it can be analyzed that majority of the Respondents that is 18(36 percentage) are sometimes clear to their duty, while 17(34 Percentage) respondents often are well aware with their duty to be performed, And only 11(22 percentage) respondents very often feel conscious regarding their work, while just 4(8 percentage) rarely feel clear regarding their duty.

Thus majority of the respondents sometimes seem to be aware to their duty.

Table.24 Showing the response of the respondents whether their personal values help them to job requirements.

Sr. NO	Particular	No of Respondents	Percentage of respondents
1	Not at all	0	0
2	Rarely	0	0
3	Sometime	7	14
4	Often	34	68
5	Very Often	9	18
	Total	50	100

your personal values help you to fulfill job requirements

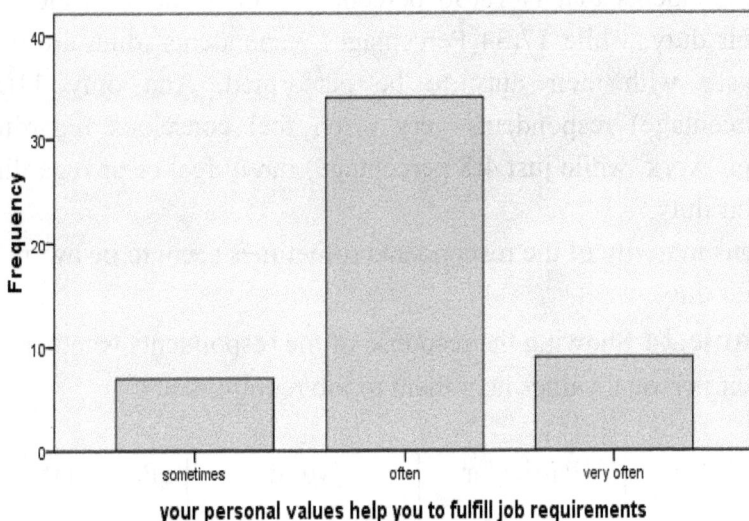

your personal values help you to fulfill job requirements

Interpretation:

From above the table it can be analyzed that majority of the Respondents that is 34(68 percentages) often feel the personal ethical values to be important, while 9 (18 Percentage) respondents very often feel the value of significance. And only 7(14percentage) respondents sometimes feel the importance of such value.

Thus majority of the respondents often give priorities to the personal values playing main role to fulfill job requirements.

Table. 25 Showing the response of the respondents whether they feel difficulties coping up with their Co-workers and supervisor due to stress associated with your job.

Sr. NO	Particular	No of Respondents	Percentage of respondents
1	Not at all	0	0
2	Rarely	0	0
3	Sometime	27	54
4	Often	7	14
5	Very Often	16	32
	Total	50	100

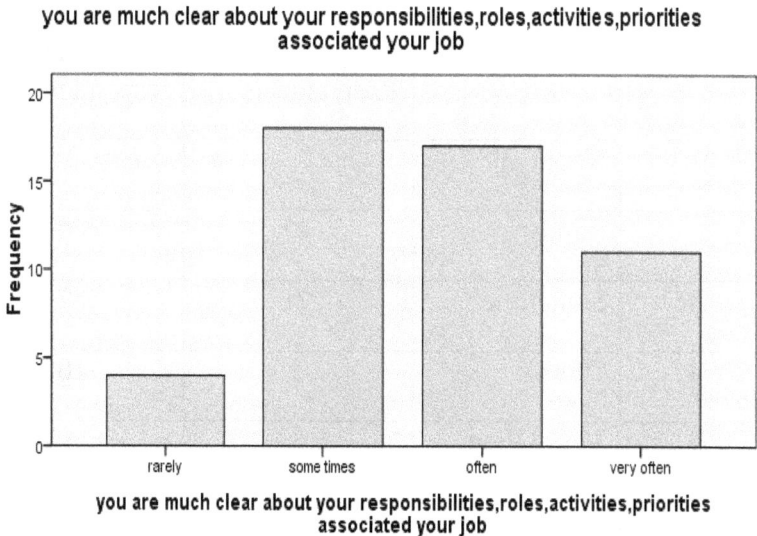

you are much clear about your responsibilities,roles,activities,priorities associated your job

Interpretation:

From above the table it can be analyzed that majority of the Respondents that is 27(54percentage) sometimes finds it difficult to adjust with their colleagues due to stress, while 16(32Percentage) respondents very often feel to be at ease with their colleagues, And only 7(14percentage) respondents often face problem while copping up with their working staff due to strenuous job.

Thus majority of the respondents sometimes find difficult to adjust with their co- workers because of stress associated with their job.

Table.26 Showing the response of the respondents whether they discuss their problem with their spouse or friend or any close mate.

Sr. NO	Particular	No of Respondents	Percentage of respondents
1	Not at all	1	2
2	Rarely	20	40
3	Sometime	21	42
4	Often	5	10
5	Very Often	3	6
	Total	50	100

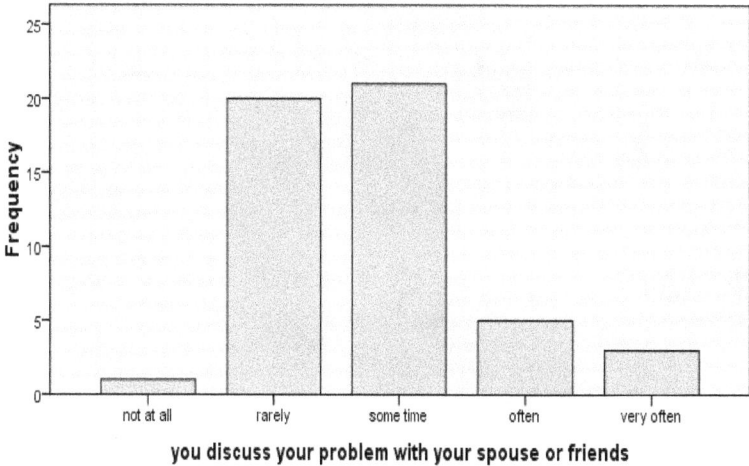

you discuss your problem with your spouse or friends

Interpretation:

From above the table it can be analyzed that majority of the Respondents that is 21(42 percentage) sometimes discuss their problem with their companions, while 20(40 Percentage) respondents rarely discuss such matters with their soul mates. And only 5(10 percentage) respondents often discuss their problems to their spouse, while just 3(6percentage) very often discuss their matters with their bosom friend, and only 1(2 percentage) never discuss their problems with their better half.

Thus majority of the respondents sometimes lessen their stress by discussing with their companions.

CHAPTER-VI

Findings, Conclusion&Suggestions

➤ Findings

Age....... From the table it can be analyzed that the majority respondents are from the middle age.(26 to 30)

Sex.......... From thetable it can be Conclude that majority 40 (80Percentage) respondents are the males, while only 10(20 Percentage) respondents are female.

Education......... From thetable it can be analyzed that majority 24(48 Percentage) respondents are graduate, while 12 (24 Percentage) respondents are only H.S.C passed, & 10(20 Percentage) respondents are only 10th passed, while 4 (8 Percentage) respondents are Post graduate.

Income...... From thetable it can be analyzed that majority, 20 (40 Percentage) respondents are getting 16000 to 20000 Rs/month, while 10 (20 Percentage) respondents are getting 12000 to 16000 Rs/month, but 10 (20 Percentage) respondents are getting only 8000 to 12000 Rs/month, and only 10 (20 Percentage) respondents are getting 20000& more Rs/month.

Work experience...: From thetable it can be analyzed that Majority 20(40 Percentage) respondents have 0 to 2 years of experience, while 15 (30 Percentage) respondents have 2 to 4 years of experience, and 6 (12Percentage) respondents have 4 to7 years of experience, and 5 (10 percentage) 7 to 10 years of experience, but only 4(8 Percentage) respondents have 10 years of experience.

✓ From the table it can be analyzed that majority of the Respondents feel the physical or emotional energy-level normal, the percentage of the rarely is 25 (50 Percentage), while only 23 (46 Percentage) respondents feel the tedium sometimes. And only 2(4 percentage) respondents feel no tedium at the work place.

   Thus majority of the respondents face the wearisome state to some rare occasions.

✓ From the table it can be analyzed that majority of the Respondents that is 42(84 percentage) feel the negative waves not at all, the percentage of the rarely is 4 (8 Percentage), while only 4 (8 Percentage) respondents feel the negative waves sometimes. And only 4(8 percentage) respondents face them sometimes at the work place.

   Thus majority of the respondents face them never.

✓ From the table it can be analyzed that majority of the Respondents that is 29(59 percentage) feel never to be misunderstood or unappreciated, and only 21 (41 Percentage), of the employee seldom feel such state.

   Thus majority of the respondents face them never.

✓ From the table it can be analyzed that majority of the Respondents that is 29 (59 percentage) miss the social networking web rarely, the percentage of feeling not at all is 21(41 Percentage),

    Thus majority of the respondents feel the lack rarely.

✓ From the table shows that majority of the Respondents that is 33(63 percentage) feel such dissatisfaction not at all, the percentage of the rarely is14 (28 Percentage), while only 3 (6 Percentage) respondents feel such state sometimes.

    Thus majority of the respondents feel such state never.

✓ From the table it can be analyzed that majority of the Respondents that is 28(56 percentage) feel the working pressure rarely. , the percentage of the employee feeling it sometimes is 15 (30 Percentage), while only 7 (14 Percentage) respondents feel it never.

    Thus majority of the respondents face them rarely.

✓ From the table it can be analyzed that majority of the Respondents that is 28(56 percentage) rarely feel the job uninteresting, the percentage feeling it sometimes is 22(44 Percentage),

    Thus majority of the respondents feels the job uninteresting rarely.

✓ From the table it can be analyzed that majority of the Respondents that is 20(40 percentage) feel such obstacle sometimes, the percentage of being felt so rarely is 15(30 Percentage), while only 15 (30 Percentage) respondents often feel such obstacle.

Thus majority of the respondents face it sometimes.

✓ From the table it can be analyzed that majority of the Respondents that is 22(44 percentage) feel such problem rarely, the percentage of facing such problem often is 18 (36 Percentage), while only 10 (20 Percentage) respondents feel the problem some times.

Thus majority of the respondents face this problem rarely.

✓ From the table it can be analyzed that majority of the Respondents that is 23(46 percentage) feel such sort of tension sometimes, the percentage of feeling it rarely is 22 (44 Percentage), while only 5 (10 Percentage) respondents often feel it .Thus majority of the respondents face such tension some times.

✓ From the table it can be analyzed that majority of the Respondents that is 29(58 percentage) is being souted by their dignitaries rarely, while 18 (36 Percentage) respondents face such scolding some times. And only 2(4 percentage) respondents face it often at the work place.

Thus majority of the respondents rarely face such problem.

✓ From the table it can be analyzed that majority of the Respondents that is 39(78 percentage) rarely face such problem, 11 (22 Percentage) of the respondents face sometimes such problems at the work place.

Thus majority of the respondents face this problem rarely.

✓ From the table it can be analyzed that majority of the Respondents that is 25(50 percentage) often takes such kind of diversion, whereas 21 (42 Percentage) respondents very often take this. And only 4(8 percentage) respondents some time take such diversion.

Thus majority of the respondents often take this sort of refreshment.

✓ From the table it can be analyzed that majority of the Respondents that is 32(64 percentage) sometimes manages to keep such balance between these two, while 17 (34 Percentage) respondents often manage to do so. And only 1(2 percentage) respondents fail to do so.

Thus majority of the respondents sometimes manage to maintain such balance.

✓ From the table it can be analyzed that majority of the Respondents that is 41(82 percentage) never feels this kind of fear, while 9 (18 Percentage) respondents rarely feel this kind of fear.

Thus majority of the respondents never feel such sort of fear.

✓ From the table it can be analyzed that majority of the Respondents that is 20(40 percentages) sometimes feels ease to attain each social function. While 16 (32 Percentage) respondents often feel comfortable to tackle the both. And only 12(24 percentage) respondents very often make it attainable, while just 2(4 percentage) rarely manage to do so.

Thus majority of the respondents sometimes finds it easy to attain it social function along with their job.

✓ From the table it can be analyzed that majority of the Respondents that is 29(58 percentage) doesn't feel irritated by small problems or by collegues. While 9(18 Percentage) respondents rarely find it easy to tackle. And only 6(12 percentage) respondents sometimes get irritated due to small blunders, while just 4(8 percentage) very often get irritated in such problems, and only 2(4 percentage) often get furiated in such situation.

Thus majority of the respondents never lose their temperament.

✓ From the table it can be analyzed that majority of the Respondents that is 18(36 percentage) are sometimes clear to their duty, while 17(34 Percentage) respondents often are well aware with their duty to be performed, And only 11(22 percentage) respondents very often feel conscious regarding their work, while just 4(8 percentage) rarely feel clear regarding their duty.

Thus majority of the respondents sometimes seem to be aware to their duty.

✓ From the table it can be analyzed that majority of the Respondents that is 34(68 percentages) often feel the personal ethical values to be important, while 9 (18 Percentage) respondents very often feel the value of significance. And only 7(14percentage) respondents sometimes feel the importance of such value.

Thus majority of the respondents often give priorities to the personal values playing main role to fulfill job requirements.

✓ From the table it can be analyzed that majority of the Respondents that is   27(54percentage) sometimes finds it difficult to adjust with their colleagues due to stress, while 16(32Percentage) respondents very often feel to be at ease with their colleagues, And only 7(14percentage) respondents often face problem while copping up with their working staff due to strenuous job.

✓ Thus majority of the respondents sometimes find difficult to adjust with their co- workers because of stress associated with their job.

✓ From the table it can be analyzed that majority of the Respondents that is 21(42 percentage) sometimes discuss their problem with their companions, while 20(40 Percentage) respondents rarely discuss such matters with their soul mates. And only 5(10 percentage) respondents often discuss their problems to their spouse, while just 3(6percentage) very often discuss their matters with their bosom friend, and only 1(2 percentage) never discuss their problems with their better half.

Thus majority of the respondents sometimes lessen their stress by discussing with their companions.

➤ Conclusion:

➤ It is concluded that majority of the Respondents feels the physical or emotional energy-level normal. Thus majority of the respondents face the wearisome state to some rare occasions.

➤ It is viewed that majority of the Respondents never feels the negative waves at work place. Thus majority of the respondents face them never.

➤ It is founded that majority of the Respondents feels never to be misunderstood or unappreciated.

➤ It is viewed that that majority of the Respondents miss the social networking web rarely. Thus majority of the respondents feel the lack rarely.

➤ It is concluded that majority of the Respondents feelsdissatisfaction not at all.   Thus majority of the respondents feel such state never.

➤ It is founded that majority of the Respondents feels the working pressure rarely.

➤ It is concluded that majority of the Respondents rarely feels the job uninteresting.

➤ It is viewed that majority of the Respondents feels obstacle sometimes.

➤ It is founded that majority of the Respondents feels sort of tension sometimes. Thus majority of the respondents face tension some times.

➤ It is viewed that majority of the Respondents are being shouted by their dignitaries rarely. Thus majority of the respondents rarely face such problem.

➤ It is founded that majority of the Respondents often takes diversion. Thus majority of the respondents often take this sort of refreshment.

➤ It is viewed that majority of the Respondents sometimes manages to keep balance between work life and social life. Thus majority of the respondents sometimes manage to maintain such balance.

➤ It is concluded that majority of the Respondents never feels accident/hazards associated with work place. Thus majority of the respondents never feel such sort of fear.

➤ It is founded that majority of the Respondents sometimes feels ease to attain each social function. Thus majority of the respondents sometimes finds it easy to attain it social function along with their job.

➢ It is concluded that majority of the Respondents doesn't feel irritated by small problems or by colleagues. Thus majority of the respondents never lose their temperament.

➢ It is viewed that majority of the Respondents are sometimes clear to their dutyto be performed. Thus majority of the respondents sometimes seem to be aware to their duty.

➢ It is founded that majority of the Respondents often feel the personal ethical values to be important. Thus majority of the respondents often give priorities to the personal values playing main role to fulfill job requirements.

➢ It is concluded that majority of the Respondents sometimes finds it difficult to adjust with their colleagues due to stress. Thus majority of the respondents sometimes find difficult to adjust with their co- workers because of stress associated with their job.

➢ It is viewed that majority of the Respondents sometimes discuss their problem with their companions. Thus majority of the respondents sometimes lessen their stress by discussing with their companions.

➢ Suggestions:

From Below Given Techniques the work stress of the middle level employees can be reduce.

➢ **Support for Managers and Employees**

The following support mechanisms are available to assist with implementation of this Strategy.

1. When you are not getting what you want out of your work situation then it's time to communicate with your employer about your wants i.e. new projects, a change of job role, an income that reflects your hard work and loyalty, training, new challenges and so on.

➢ **Corporate Training and Development (CTD)**

CTD provide a range of courses that can help managers and individual employees address potential causes of stress and help individuals deal effectively with work pressures, for example:

- Developing and managing employee performance
- Handling difficult situations assertively
- Dealing with violence and aggression
- Customer care
- Individual well-being
- Sickness absence management (Improving Attendance)

➢ Human Resources (HR), Personnel

To provide support and guidance to managers and employees in dealing with stress and in the use of the Council's related policies and procedures, for example:

○ **Work-life balance (WLB): -** Personal issues may reduce the individual's ability to cope with normal work pressures and vice versa. This may lead to their performance suffering, sickness absence, etc. Therefore, even if the primary cause is not work appropriate support should be provided to the employee. This support may include looking at how the organization can help the employee achieve a better work-life balance.

The Department for Trade and Industry website gives the following definition of WLB: 'Work-life balance is about adjusting working patterns. Regardless of age, race or gender, everyone can find a rhythm to help them combine work with their other responsibilities or aspirations'.

• Lack of sleep can heavily impact your ability to view things objectively. If you are not getting enough sleep then your perspective in life will be distorted to such an extent that you are not seeing things clearly, are probably not very productive and you are definitely adding to your stress levels at work and home.

• Watch your intake of "uppers" and "downers" – that means coffee, cola drinks, tea and chocolate bars or refined & processed foods (uppers) and heavy carbohydrate meals like cooked chips, burgers, fried foods (downers). While carbohydrates give you energy – there is very little value in these processed versions. The lower you feel the more likely you are to go in search of highs and so the see-saw gains its momentum.

- Watch out for work addiction – it's real, it goes unnoticed (and is often rewarded) and it damages health, relationships, families, self-esteem and motivation. Like other addicts, the workaholic is using their job to busy themselves as a way of denying or squashing pain or "holes" they feel in other parts of their lives or themselves. Work holism is extremely destructive and in some cases has lead to suicide. Look out for it in yourself, your colleagues, friends and family – and most of all watch that you are not encouraging it in your staff.

Appendix
INTERVIEW SCHEDULE

"A STUDY ON EMPLOYEE WORKPLACE SRTESS"

(A study of Middle level Employees of Sabar Dairy, Himatnagar)

Personal Information:

1) Name   :

2) Age   : [ ] 18-25   [ ] 26-35   [ ] 36-50 [ ] 50 above

3) Sex   : [ ] Male   [ ] Female

4) Educational qualification : [ ] S.S.C.   [ ] H.S.C [ ] Graduate   [ ] Post Graduate

5) Current Designation   :

6) Income per-month   : [ ]3000-5000   [ ]5100-7000[ ] 7100-10,000[ ]10,000 above

7) Work Experience   : [ ] 0-2 years [ ]3-4 years[ ]5-7 years[ ]8-10 years[ ]10ye. above

8) Department   :

9) Date of joining   :

10) Number of promotion   :

11) Number of transfer   :

                                   Signature

The Information collected from the respondents will be kept highly confidential & will be used for research purpose only.

Questionnaire						
No	Questions	Not at all	Rarely	Sometimes	Often	Very often
1	Do you feel run down and drained of physical or emotional energy at your work?					
2	Do you feel Negative waves at your work place?					
3	Do you feel you are misunderstood or unappreciated by your co-workers and / or Supervisor?					
4	Are you missing social networking at your work place?					
5	Do you feel that whatever you have achieved is less than your capacity due to work stress?					
6	Do you feel an unpleasant level of pressure at your work to get work					

	done?				
7	Do you think that the job has been given to you is not of your area of interest?				
8	Do you feel that due to heavy load of work you haven't any extra time to spend for personal development?				
9	Do you feel that due to heavy load of work you haven't time to maintain quality of your job?				
10	Do you get frustration/ tension for non-achievement of your target?				
11	Do your Supervisor or Boss sout on you due to poor performance?				

12	Does your work load force you to work beyond working hours?					
13	Do you take support of entertainment to kill work stress?					
14	Do you usually get success to have balance between work life and social life?					
15	Do you feel fear of accident/hazards associated with your work place?					
16	Does your job allow you to attain each social function?					
17	Do you find yourself getting easily irritate by small problems, or by your co-workers and team?					

18	Are you much clear about your responsibilities, roles, activities, priorities associated with your job?					
19	Do you feel that your personal values help you to fulfill job requirements?					
20	Do you find yourself harder and less sympathetic towards your Co-workers and supervisor due to stress associated with your job?					
21	Do you discuss your problem with your spouse or friend or any other close to you?					

Bibliography

Ajai Thomas : A Study of Organizational work place Stress and leadership in 2004 IDMC LTD.

Chartered Society of Physiotherapy, Employment Relations &Union Services: Health & Safety – Workplace Stress, CSP, 2004

Clifford T. Margan : Introduction to psychology, first Edition 1974,Tata McGraw-Hill Publishing Company.

History and Present status concept 1991 – Columbia University Press

HSE, A business case for the Management Standards for Stress, HSE Books, 2006

MIND, 'Stress and mental health in the workplace', Mindweek report, May 2005

National Institute for Occupational Safety and Health, Stress at Work, U.S. Department of Health andHuman Services, 1999

Oxford Dictionary English to English and Latin – 2005

Palmer S, Cooper C and Thomas K, 'Model of organizational stress for use within an occupational health education/promotion or wellbeing programme – A short communication', Health EducationJournal, Vol. 60 No.4, 2001

Parikh Udai : Instruments of Human Resource Development & Organizational Development, second Edition 2007, Tata McGraw-Hill Publishing Company.

Shefaly Shah : Organization & work stress in Hindalco Industries Ltd., 1995

➢ Websites
1. http://www.stress.org.uk
2. http://www.isma.org.uk
3. http://www.workstress.net
4. http://www.cipd.co.uk
5. http://www.biomedcentral.com
6. http://www.stress.lovetoknow.com

www.ingramcontent.com/pod-product-compliance
Lightning Source LLC
Chambersburg PA
CBHW060623210326
41520CB00010B/1449